MICHAEL DUCKWORTH

Going International

English for Tourism

Workbook

OXFORD UNIVERSITY PRESS 1998

425. 910179   1/05

33875

Oxford University Press
Great Clarendon Street, Oxford OX2 6DP

Athens   Auckland   Bangkok   Bogota
Buenos Aires   Calcutta   Cape Town   Chennai
Dar es Salaam   Delhi   Florence   Hong Kong
Istanbul   Karachi   Kuala Lumpur   Madrid
Melbourne   Mexico City   Mumbai   Nairobi
Paris   Sao Paulo   Singapore   Taipei   Tokyo
Toronto   Warsaw

and associated companies in
Berlin   Ibadan

OXFORD and OXFORD ENGLISH
are trade marks of Oxford University Press

ISBN 0 19 457402 4

© Oxford University Press 1998

Printed in Spain

Acknowledgements

*The author and publisher are grateful to those who have given
permission to reproduce the following extracts from and adaptations
of copyright material:*

p12 Statistics reprinted by permission of the Statistics &
Research Division of the Tourism Authority of Thailand;
p14 'An insider's secrets to becoming a flight attendant'
by permission of the Flight Corporation of America;
p20 Virgin Atlantic; *pp34–5* P&O Cruises for extracts from
1997 brochure (2nd edition); *p38* Yacht Connections, Ltd.;
p48 Thomson Holidays for extract from Thomson Faraway
Shores 1997/98 brochure; *p49* KLM for flight information
(please note that this flight information is only intended as an
example); *p53* Crescentcity.com website Copyright © 1997
Ambush, Inc.; *p55* Information from IPC's Travelbase web site
reprinted by permission of Travelbase; *p60* Titan Travel Limited
for extracts from the Titan HiTours 1998 brochure; *p63* The
Tower of London by Peter Hammond, by permission of the
Historic Royal Palaces Agency (crown copyright: Historic Royal
Palaces); *p64* 'American Marketing Disasters' from the Auto
Channel web site by permission of The Auto Channel;
p68 Exodus Travels Ltd. for extracts from the Exodus Walking
Holidays Brochure 1997/98; *p70* 'Space Hotel' by Dr Roger
Highfield, with his permission.

Illustrations by:

Brett Breckon   *pp39, 70*
Neil Gower   *pp31, 50, 55, 60*
Barrie Mitchell   *pp51, 73*
Harry Venning   *pp30, 36, 44*

*The Publisher would like to thank the following for their permission
to reproduce photographs:*

Bridgeman Art Library *p59* Tower of London from the
East, (aquatint) by Thomas Daniell (1749-1840) & William
(1769-1837) Guildhall Library, Corporation of London, *p63*
The Princes Edward and Richard in the Tower, 1483 by Sir John
Everett Millais (1829-96) Royal Holloway and Bedford New
College, Surrey, British Crown Jewels, Illustrated London
News; Corbis UK Ltd., *p53* Confederate Museum, Longue Vue
House/Robert Holmes; Getty Images, *p4* the Eiffel Tower, Big Ben,
the Parthenon, the Statue of Liberty, the Coliseum, *p38* scuba
diving; Crown Copyright: Historic Royal Palaces, *p63* Chapel of
St John; Link/Images of India, *p8* Thaipusam Festival/Eric
Meacher; James Davis Travel Photography, *p38* beach –
St Vincent, Union Island – anchored ship, *p68* trekking in the
Annapurna region; Nancy Robert, *p53* Destrehane Plantation;
Pictor International, *p4* Sydney Opera House, *p11* Rollercoaster
World, *p12* Wat Arun statue – Bangkok, *p42* Kuala Lumpur
railway; The Imagebank, *p5* female portrait; Thomas Cook
Archives, *p7* Cooks Tours; Thomson Tour Operations Ltd.,
p14 flight attendant, *p47* Penang Mutiara beach resort.

Although every effort has been made to trace and contact
copyright holders, this has not always been possible. If notified
the publisher will be pleased to rectify any errors or omissions at
the earliest opportunity.

Contents

1

The history and development of tourism

1

Sights and cities

What are the names of these famous sights and cities, and where can they be found? The words below are mixed up. Reorder the letters to find the answers. The first one has been done for you.

Famous sights

eeffil eortw
aciloopsr
gbi neb
aesttu fo beilrty
aeopr ehosu
celmoossu

Cities

dlnnoo
ndesyy
aehnst
aiprs
enw kory
emor

1

Name   *Eiffel Tower*
City   *Paris*

2

Name _____
City _____

3

Name _____
City _____

4

Name _____
City _____

5

Name _____
City _____

6

Name _____
City _____

2   Likes and dislikes

Read the following passage in which Margarita Martinez talks about her job.

MARGARITA MARTINEZ

I work for a large tour operator, and part of my job is to try out new holiday destinations, cruises, and so on. The best thing about my job is that I get the chance to travel abroad, and I also meet new people, which I think is fantastic. I've been on lots of trips, but my favourite one last year was a river cruise down the Nile to Karnak – I think ancient Egypt is so fascinating. Normally I don't really look forward to going on cruises because I get so seasick, but I find flying OK most of the time. The only time I don't is when I have to go on really long flights – and I can tell you, going from Madrid to Australia is terrible!

A Write sentences about her likes and dislikes using the verbs in brackets. The first one has been done for you .

1 (love)   _She loves travelling abroad._ _____

2 (love)   _____

3 (interested)   _____

4 (dislike)   _____

5 (not mind)   _____

6 (hate)   _____

B Now write a short paragraph saying what you like and dislike about your work, studies, or a holiday job you have had.

_____

_____

_____

_____

_____

3   Simple past and present perfect

A Read the following sentences. Put a tick (✔) next to the sentences that are correct. Put a cross (✗) next to the sentences that have a mistake and put them right. The first two have been done for you.

1 I have never been to Italy. ✔

2 My brother is in England since July. ✗ _My brother **has been** in England ..._

3 Manuel has finished his diploma in tourism last year.

4 My family lived in India for two years, and then we went to Japan.

5 The agent says she has sent you the tickets yesterday.

6 She doesn't work for TWA any more – she's been with Qantas for last May.

7 Have you ever been to South America?

8 My father has learned a little English when he was at school.

9 I have just finished my course and I am looking for a job.

10 I have worked for Jaybee Travel since two years.

11 The flight didn't arrive yet.

B Sally Ray is being interviewed for a job in a travel agency. Read through this extract from her interview. Put the verbs in brackets into the present perfect or simple past. The first one has been done for you.

INTERVIEWER   I'd like to talk about your work experience. [1] _Have you ever worked_ (you/ever/work) in the travel business before?

SALLY   Yes, so far I [2] _____ (have) two jobs related to tourism. I [3] _____ (work) for Solarvil two years ago, and I [4] _____ (be) responsible for looking after clients renting their villas and houses.

INTERVIEWER   And [5] _____ (you/enjoy) it?

SALLY   Yes, I [6] _____ (love) it, but it [7] _____ (be) only a summer job. And the following year – last year – I [8] _____ (go) to their Morocco office to do the same sort of thing.

INTERVIEWER   I see. Now, there is something that I have to ask you. Solarvil obviously think you're good because they [9] _____ (give) you jobs over the last two years – [10] _____ (you/apply) to work with them this summer as well?

SALLY   Yes, but I [11] _____ (only just/send off) the application form, and I [12] _____ (not/receive) a reply yet. And anyway, I [13] _____ (always/think) that it was a good idea to look at new opportunities, and that's why I [14] _____ (decide) to get in touch with you.

4 Vocabulary   Tourism and travel

A Put the words from the list into the correct boxes below. Some words may appear in more than one box. See the examples.

airline	_art gallery_	beach	boarding card
charter flight	check-in desk	currency	departure lounge
excursion	foreign exchange	in-flight magazine	insurance policy
museum	passenger	plane	price war
railway	sightseeing	stagecoach	tour guide
tourist	train	road	travel agent
traveller's cheques			

Money	Tourism	People & jobs

Tourist attractions	Air travel	Other transport
art gallery	airline	

B Answer the following questions using your own ideas. Each answer must contain two words or phrases from a box on page 6. The first one has been done for you.

1 Is there still time to check in for BA 663?

Yes, but you'll have to go straight to the departure lounge because the plane is about to leave.

2 Is there anything I ought to visit while I'm in the city?

_____

3 Can you organize some money for me to take to Mexico?

_____

4 Do most people go round the city on their own or do they have someone to show them round?

_____

5 How will I be able to get to the capital if the air traffic controllers' strike goes ahead?

_____

6 Why did the plane leave so late?

_____

5 Reading   Around the world in 222 days

Read the text and complete the exercises that follow.

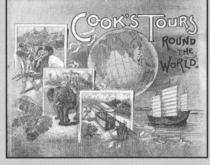

The history of modern tourism began on 5 July 1841, when a train carrying 500 factory workers travelled from Leicester to Loughborough, twelve miles away, to attend a meeting about the dangers of alcohol.

This modest excursion was organized by Thomas Cook, a young man with neither money nor formal education. His motive was not profit, but social reform. Cook believed that the social problems of Britain were caused by widespread alcoholism. Travel, he believed, would broaden the mind and distract people from drinking.

The success of Cook's first excursion led to others, and the success of the business was phenomenal. In 1851, Cook launched his own monthly newsletter, Cook's *Exhibition Herald and Excursion Advertiser*, the world's first travel magazine; by 1872, the newsletter was selling 100,000 copies a month and its founder was treated as a hero of the modern industrial age.

When Thomas Cook reached the age of sixty-three, there was still one challenge ahead of him: to travel round the globe. The idea of travelling 'to Egypt via China' seemed impossible to most Victorians. Cook knew otherwise. In 1869 two things happened that would make an overland journey possible: the opening of the Suez Canal and the completion of a railroad network that linked the continent of America from coast to coast.

He set off from Liverpool on the steamship *Oceanic*, bound for New York. Throughout his travels, his traditional views affected most of what he saw, including the American railroad system. Although impressed by its open carriages, sleeping cars, on-board toilets and efficient baggage handling, he was shocked that men and women were not required to sleep in separate carriages.

Japan delighted him. It was a land of 'great beauty and rich fertility,' where the hotels served 'the best roast beef we have tasted since we left England'. Cook and his party toured the city of Yokohama in a caravan of rickshaws. 'We created quite a sensation,' he wrote.

Cook's love of Japan was equalled only by his hatred of China. Shanghai, the next port of call, offered 'narrow and filthy streets' which were full of 'pestering and festering beggars'. After twenty-four hours there, Cook had seen enough.

He travelled to Singapore and as he set off across the Bay of Bengal, Cook was full of confidence, feeling that he understood 'this business of pleasure'. But nothing he had seen in Shanghai could have prepared him for the culture shock of India.

'At the holy city of Benares we were conducted through centres of filth and obscenity,' he wrote. From the deck of a boat on the Ganges he saw the people washing dead bodies, before burning them on funeral piles beside the river. He found these scenes 'revolting in the extreme'.

By the time Cook left Bombay for Egypt, he was showing signs of tiredness. On 15 February 1873, while crossing the Red Sea, he wrote to *The Times* that he would not travel round the world again. 'After thirty-two years of travelling, with the view of making travelling easy, cheap, and safe for others, I ought to rest.' In Cairo, he fell seriously ill for the first time.

Cook arrived home in England after 222 days abroad. Although he never attempted another world tour, he continued to escort parties of tourists to continental Europe throughout the 1870s, and did not cease his seasonal visits to Egypt until the late 1880s. He died in July 1892 at the age of eighty-three.

A Are the following statements true (T) or false (F)?

1 Cook organized his first tour in order to make some money.
2 He launched the world's first travel magazine in 1872.
3 The Suez Canal was opened in 1869.
4 He thought some aspects of the American railroad system were excellent.
5 He preferred China to Japan.
6 He was shocked by what he saw in India.
7 He fell ill towards the end of his round-the-world tour.
8 He handed the business over to his son when he was sixty-five.

B Itinerary

The following place names are mixed up. Reorder the letters to find the words and write the place names in the order that Cook visited them. The first one has been done for you.

Bya fo BagIne	Bersean	1 _Liverpool_	7 _____
Sapierogn	Bmoyab	2 _____	8 _____
Lerolovpi	Shaiagnh	3 _____	9 _____
Crioa	Nwe Ykro	4 _____	10 _____
Egdnaln	Jnpaa	5 _____	11 _____
Rde Sae		6 _____	

6 Simple present active or passive

Read this extract from a hotel information brochure. Put the verbs in brackets into the simple present active or passive. The first one has been done for you.

The Hindu festival of Thaipusam is one of Malaysia's most famous and colourful festivals, and ceremonies

1 _are held_ (hold) **in temples all over the country in honour of the Hindu god Subramaniam.**

The devotees* who 2_____ (want) to take part in the festival 3_____ (eat) special food for several weeks before Thaipusam so that their bodies will be prepared. When the day 4_____ (arrive), they go into a temple, where special chants 5_____ (sing) by a priest. The devotees go into a trance, and the priest 6_____ (push) long metal rods through their cheeks, nose, or tongue. Sometimes hooks 7_____ (attach) to their backs, and they 8_____ (pull) a kind of cart, which 9_____ (call) a *kavadi*, along the street. At other temples, fire-walking ceremonies 10_____ (organize), and the devotees 11_____ (walk) several metres over red hot coal. Perhaps the most astonishing thing about these ceremonies is that the devotees 12_____ (not/harm) in any way. There is no blood, and the cuts 13_____ (heal) very quickly.

Thaipusam 14_____ (take) place early in the year, and this year it falls on 28 January. One of the best places to see the ceremonies is at the Batu Caves, which 15_____ (situated) only a few miles from Kuala Lumpur. Transport to the caves can 16_____ (arrange) by the hotel.

devotees* = people who take part in the ceremony

7 Writing

Describing a festival

Write a similar description of a festival for a hotel information brochure. Choose a festival that you know about, or use the notes below about the Edinburgh Festival. Divide your passage into three main paragraphs.

1 Give a very short introduction, saying what the festival is.
2 Give a more detailed description of what happens during the festival.
3 Give some practical information that a tourist would need to know.

The Edinburgh Festival

- Edinburgh Festival – Scotland
- international artists
- August/September ever year
- series of French films
- New York Symphony orchestra – Beethoven's 9th
- available at hotel – programmes, tickets

- travel arrangements – see reception
- festival plays, concerts, exhibitions
- started 1947
- this year – Royal Ballet, *Swan Lake*
- new plays from around the world
- early booking essential for some shows

8 Review

Look back at the unit. Write eight true sentences using words from each column and the simple past passive. The first one has been done for you.

a	b	c
Laker Airways	design	César Manrique
The first Olympics	build	Thomas Cook
César Manrique	paint	Leonardo da Vinci
The Suez Canal	open	Ancient Egyptians
The first package tours	organize	Arrecife
The Jardin de Cactus	hold	776 BC
The Pyramids	be born	*1966*
The Mona Lisa	*found*	1869

1 *Laker Airways was founded in 1966.*
2 _____
3 _____
4 _____
5 _____
6 _____
7 _____
8 _____

2

The organization and structure of tourism

2   **1**   **Question forms**

A consultant is interviewing a passenger in the departure lounge at Changi Airport in Singapore. Read the passenger's replies and work out what the questions were. The first one has been done for you.

INTERVIEWER   Excuse me, sir, would you mind answering some questions about the level of service you have received at the airport?

PASSENGER   No, not at all. My flight doesn't leave for twenty minutes.

INTERVIEWER   Thank you. (travel/airport) [1] _How did you travel to the airport_ ?

PASSENGER   I came by taxi.

INTERVIEWER   (how long/wait/check in) [2] _____ ?

PASSENGER   Only five minutes or so. It was very efficient.

INTERVIEWER   (any problems/finding your way around) [3] _____ ?

PASSENGER   No, I didn't have any at all – everything was very clear.

INTERVIEWER   (airline/fly) [4] _____ ?

PASSENGER   With Singapore Airlines.

INTERVIEWER   (you/go) [5] _____ ?

PASSENGER   I'm going to Amsterdam.

INTERVIEWER   (travel/business/holiday) [6] _____ ?

PASSENGER   I'm travelling on business, but I'm hoping to have a few days' holiday as well.

INTERVIEWER   (use/duty-free shop) [7] _____ ?

PASSENGER   Yes, I have. I bought some whisky and some cigars.

INTERVIEWER   (other airport facilities/use) [8] _____ ?

PASSENGER   None. Oh, wait a minute, I used the bank to change some money.

INTERVIEWER   (any improvements/like to see) [9] _____ ?

PASSENGER   Yes, I'd love to see some signs in Dutch, but I don't suppose that's very likely.

Indirect questions

A passenger at an airport is being asked about his hotel arrangements. Rephrase the interviewer's questions beginning with the polite phrases in brackets. The first one has been done for you.

1 Which hotel will you be staying at? (*Could you tell me ...?*)
   Could you tell me which hotel you will be staying at?

2 Have you ever been there before? (*May I ...?*)
   _____

3 Did anyone recommend it to you? (*Can you ...?*)
   _____

4 Why did you choose it? (*Would you mind ...?*)
   _____

5 How much does it cost? (*Could you ...?*)
   _____

6 What facilities does it have? (*Can you ...?*)
   _____

7 Does the hotel have a courtesy bus? (*May I ...?*)
   _____

8 When will you be leaving? (*Would you mind ...?*)
   _____

3 The language of graphs

Read the report about the number of visitors at Rollercoaster World, a major tourist attraction, over the year. Then use the information to complete the bar chart below.

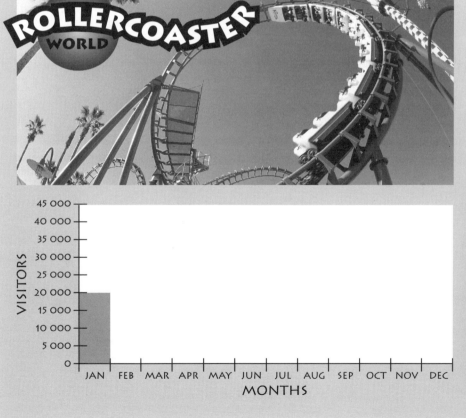

There were 20,000 visitors in January, although most of these came just after New Year and before the new school term. In February there was a sharp fall to 5,000 but this rose by 2,000 in March as the weather improved. In April numbers rose by 5,000 and there was a gradual increase in May and June, when numbers went up by 3,000 each month and then levelled off in June. The most popular month was August, when numbers more than doubled to 40,000 because of the school holidays and the summer tourist season, and there was a sharp fall of 10,000 in September. Numbers fell gradually during October and November by 5,000 a month, and then levelled off at 20,000 in December.

Read the following information. Complete the pie chart below and put the missing figures in the table.

International tourist arrivals to Thailand

January – December

country of origin	no. of tourists	%
East Asia (excluding ASEAN*)	2,794,149	38.85
ASEAN Countries	1,689,434	
Europe	1,605,287	22.32
The Americas	384,060	5.34
Others	719,214	10.00
Grand total	**7,192,144**	**100**

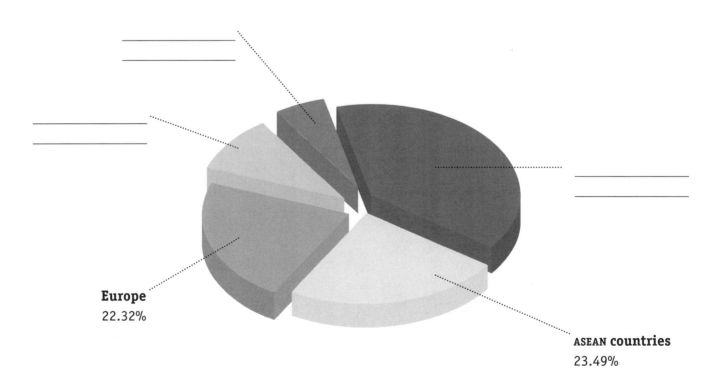

_____

_____

_____

_____

_____

_____

Europe
22.32%

ASEAN countries
23.49%

* ASEAN – The Association of South East Asian Nations

5 Vocabulary — Jobs in tourism

1	C u r a t o r
2	
3	
4	
5	
6	
7	
8	
9	

Complete the wordsquare to find the missing word. The clues are listed below. The first one has been done for you.

1 The _curator_ of the museum is planning a big new exhibition for next spring. (7)

2 These bags are terribly heavy. Do you know where I can find a _____ to help me? (6)

3 The air traffic _____ gave the plane permission to take off. (9)

4 After I had collected my luggage, a _____ officer asked me to open one of my suitcases. (7)

5 The _____ informed the passengers that they would be landing in twenty minutes. (5)

6 During the flight, the _____ came round with the drinks trolley. (10)

7 If you have lost something on the train, the _____ may be able to help you. (5)

8 When the plane landed, the _____ handlers unloaded the hold. (7)

9 Room 235 has not been prepared yet. Could you send a _____ to clean it up? (11)

6 Vocabulary — Sectors of the tourism industry

A Look at the different sectors of the tourism industry below. In each box, write four jobs that are related to it. See the example.

Accommodation	Tourist attractions	Finance
chambermaid		

Training establishments	Tourist organizations	Carriers

B Write sentences describing two jobs you have noted down in each of the boxes. See the example.

1 _In a hotel, a chambermaid cleans the rooms and the receptionist greets guests when they arrive._

2 _____

3 _____

4 _____

5 _____

6 _____

Becoming a flight attendant

The following text is an extract from the book *An insider's secrets to becoming a flight attendant*. It contains examples of questions currently being asked at job interviews for flight attendants and model answers. Below is a list of the questions which have been removed from the extract. Put them in the correct space in the text. The first one has been done for you.

a Give an example of a recent situation in which you disagreed with a co-worker and how you handled it.
b Tell us about yourself.
c How do you feel about having to conform to our uniform standards?
d Why do you want to leave your current employer?
e What do you think is the primary responsibility of a flight attendant?
f How many days of work did you miss due to illness last year?
g What is my name?
h *Why do you want to be a flight attendant for our airline?*

1 _Why do you want to be a flight attendant for our airline?_

This question is often asked at a first interview with the airlines. Try to answer in terms of what you can do for the airline, rather than what the airline can do for you. You don't want to state 'because of the travel benefits' or 'because of all the time off.'

2 _____

This is also a common question during the first interview. Try to have a clear, concise statement prepared, but don't have it completely memorized so it sounds like a canned speech. You don't have to start at birth and work forward. You can use the following list as a guideline to help you. You can state your name, where you grew up, your education/training (including any languages you speak), your current job title and responsibilities, previous experience (preferably in the customer service field), volunteer work/hobbies, extracurricular activities/honors, or anything else that makes you unique.

3 _____

Safety. Providing comfort and service to the passengers are secondary duties.

4 _____

Conformity is very important to airlines. It's important to express complete compliance with any of their rules and regulations.

5 _____

Show your maturity and ability to get along with others. They are looking for someone who can confront an individual in a diplomatic manner and get the problem resolved. There are no supervisors at 10,000 metres!

6 _____

This is a test of your listening skills. If possible, write down who is interviewing you when you are introduced. It is also a bonus to remember the information, so after the interview you can thank them (remember to use Mr, Mrs, or Ms). They will be impressed with your memory and your professionalism.

7 _____

Don't state the negatives concerning your current job. Instead you can reiterate your strong desire to pursue a career as a flight attendant.

8 _____

Attendance is a very important issue in the airline industry due to the nature of the job. They are looking for people who will provide near perfect attendance, and who can demonstrate a good attendance record in the past.

Source– Flight Attendant Corporation Of America, P.O. Box 260803, Littleton, CO 80163

The PRINCESSA HOTEL group

This highly prestigious international hotel group, with luxury four-star hotels in fifteen world capitals, seeks to recruit dedicated professionals for **junior management** positions in our establishments in Europe, Asia, and South America.

We are looking for candidates with at least two years' experience in a relevant environment, excellent language and communication skills, and a passion for excellence.

Outstanding salary and benefits package. Please apply in writing to: **Alfredo Rodriguez, Operations Manager, The Hotel Princessa, PO Box 233456, New York, USA**

A When you apply for a job, it is usual to send a covering letter with your CV. Here is the covering letter sent by an applicant for a job as junior manager in a big international hotel chain. The sentences are in the wrong order. Decide which is the right order and write the letter out in full.

a I am now seeking a post that will offer me greater responsibility and the opportunity to develop my management skills.

b Dear Mr Rodriguez

c I do hope that you will consider inviting me for interview, and I look forward to hearing from you.

d Besides my good general background in different aspects of hotel management, I also have a particular interest in computer accounting systems (see attached CV), speak fluent German and English, and intermediate-level Spanish.

e I am enthusiastic and hard-working and would enjoy the challenge of working to maintain high standards in a top-class hotel.

f I am writing in reply to your advertisement in the International Gazette, on Tuesday 14th November, for junior managers with the Princessa Hotel Group.

g Having worked successfully in a range of posts of increasing responsibility, from chambermaid, to switchboard operator, to front desk receptionist, I have gained a wide range of experience and overall hands-on knowledge of the day-to-day running of a hotel.

h Please find enclosed my CV with full details of my qualifications and experience to date.

i As you will see from my CV, I graduated from the University of Brighton with a Diploma in Hotel Management and Catering, and have had nearly four years' experience in different types of hotel work in Germany, Austria, and Mallorca, as well as in Britain.

j Yours sincerely
Ulrike Christiansen

B Look at the list of tips for writing good covering letters below. Choose the right words from the box to complete them.

achievements	repeat	summarize	interview
address	experience	where	when

1 A good covering letter should not _____ the information given on your CV but should _____ it.

2 If the job advertisement contains a contact name, it is polite to _____ your letter to that person: *Dear Mr Rodriguez, Dear Ms Leone*, etc.

3 Start your letter by stating clearly which job you are applying for, and _____ and _____ you saw the advertisement for it.

4 The main body of the letter should contain a summary of your relevant _____ and/or any abilities or _____ which you think it would be useful to mention: remember you are trying to impress!

5 Finish your letter by saying what you feel you could bring to the company. Make sure you indicate your willingness to attend an _____.

C Find an advertisement for a job in tourism that interests you (or use the one above). Write the covering letter that you would send with your CV if you were applying for this job.

3

Travel agents

1 Vocabulary   Holiday types

A In the centre below is a list of different types of holiday. Match each holiday type with the correct set of words in the boxes. See the example.

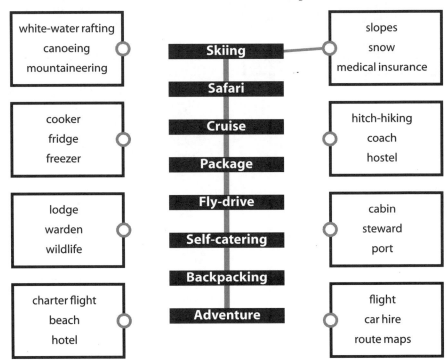

white-water rafting canoeing mountaineering	**Skiing**	slopes snow medical insurance
	Safari	
cooker fridge freezer	**Cruise**	hitch-hiking coach hostel
	Package	
lodge warden wildlife	**Fly-drive** **Self-catering**	cabin steward port
	Backpacking	
charter flight beach hotel	**Adventure**	flight car hire route maps

B Choose two types of holiday and word sets. Write down what you might say to a customer about the holiday using all the words in each set. See the example.

We have some very good skiing holidays on offer in Obergurgl – it's very high so you're guaranteed to have snow on the slopes, and we can also offer very good rates for additional medical insurance.

1 _____

_____

_____

2 _____

_____

_____

Taking a booking

A customer is ringing a travel agent to book a flight. Number the dialogue in the correct order. The first one has been done for you.

JANE   That's right. How can I help you, sir? ___

JANE   Good morning. This is Star Travel. Jane speaking. _1_

JANE   Goodbye. ___

JANE   Certainly. I'll just give you the booking reference number. It's LF2254G. ___

JANE   It leaves at 6.30 and arrives at 8.00. Would that suit you? ___

JANE   I'm not sure. I'll check availability for you. Do you have a preference for any particular airline? ___

JANE   Do you want to confirm it? ___

JANE   OK. Now, let me see … there's availability on the 18th on an early morning flight with Lufthansa. ___

ALAN   Yes, that would be fine. ___

ALAN   I'd prefer British Airways or Lufthansa. ___

ALAN   Yes, please, and could you charge it to our account? ___

ALAN   How early? ___

ALAN   Hello, this is Alan March from GKC. We have an account with you. ___

ALAN   I'd like to book a flight to Munich on the 18th of November. Do you think there will be any seats left? ___

ALAN   LF2254G. OK, thanks very much. Goodbye. ___

Making suggestions

Look through the different expressions we can use to make suggestions.

What about …		You could …	
How about …	going by train?	Why don't you …	go by train.
Have you thought of …		If I were you I'd …	

Now read the following questions asked by customers in a travel agency. Make suggestions and add some extra information. Use the words in brackets in your answer. The first one has been done for you.

1 I've got to go to Paris this week, but I'm a bit worried about the air traffic controllers going on strike. (ferry/comfortable/sailings)
   Have you thought of going by ferry? It's very comfortable and there are lots of sailings.

2 I'd like to drive around Spain, but I don't really want to take my own car. (hire a car/good value/book in advance)

___

3 My daughter wants to travel round Europe for a few weeks. What is the best way of getting around? (Inter-rail card/valid 1 month/go wherever she likes)

___

4 Do you know any hotels near the airport that I can stay in? (Sheraton/five minutes from Terminal 2/free courtesy bus)

___

5 I'd love to go to Greece, but I'm worried it might be too hot. (spring/weather lovely/not too crowded)

___

6 Where can I take my six-year-old son for the holiday of a lifetime?
(Disneyland® Paris/easy to reach/very popular with children)

_____

7 I'd like to see a bit of the city but I haven't got much time. What can I do?
(bus tour/very interesting/two hours)

_____

4 Vocabulary

Business travel

A travel agent is talking to a client about business travel. Fill in the blanks using a word from column **A** and a word from column **B**. The first one has been done for you.

A		B	
express	corporate	service	rooms
incentive	fax	check-in	machine
limousine	meeting	leg-room	bar
automatic	mini	upgrade	hall
extra	modem	scheme	discount
conference		point	

'I would certainly recommend East American Airlines if you're going to be doing a lot of travelling in the States – they like to make things easy. For a start, they offer a free chauffeur-driven [1] _limousine_ _service_ to take you to the airport and to pick you up the other end, and they have an [2] _____ _____ solely for the use of passengers in Business Class, so you only have to get there ten minutes before the flight. What's more, you also have the chance of an [3] _____ _____ to First Class if there are any free seats. The planes are very comfortable – the seats have lots of [4] _____ _____ so you don't feel cramped, and they offer a good range of meals on the menu. On top of that there is an air miles [5] _____ _____, so that if you fly with them regularly, you can quickly earn enough points for a free flight.

In Georgia, they have an arrangement with the Eastern Traveler's Inn, which has been specially built to meet the needs of the business traveller. It's in a good area of town, and the rooms are very nice. They all have a [6] _____ _____ with snacks as well as drinks, and they come with a [7] _____ _____ so that you can get your e-mail from a portable PC, and they also have a [8] _____ _____ so that you can send and receive other documents. If you want to give a small presentation, you can hire one of the [9] _____ _____ which can hold up to twenty people, but if you're planning something big, like a product launch for example, you can hire the [10] _____ _____ , which can seat over 1,000. It's very good value, but for regular guests they also offer a [11] _____ _____ of about thirty per cent.'

5   Obligation and necessity

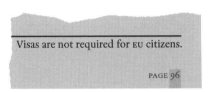

1 <u>*You aren't allowed to park here.*</u>

BAGGAGE MUST NOT BE LEFT UNATTENDED AT ANY TIME.

2 _____

Visas are not required for EU citizens.

PAGE 96

3 _____

DUTY FREE ALLOWANCES
CIGARETTES **200**

4 _____

Read the signs and notices. Rewrite each item in less formal language, as if you were talking to someone and explaining what it means. Use the expressions in the box. The first one has been done for you.

you can/can't	you don't have to	you have to
you are/aren't allowed to	you don't need to	you've got to

SMOKING AREA

BALANCE DUE BY...   29 June 1997

5 _____   7 _____

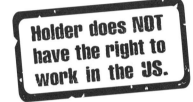

Holder does NOT have the right to work in the US.

Flight	From
BAT4572	NEW YORK
Date	Destination
28JUL	LONDON HEATHROW

NOT TRANSFERABLE

6 _____   8 _____

6   Telephone language

Read through the following conversation. Choose the correct option from the words in italics. The first one has been done for you.

A   Good morning. Mediterranean World. Can I help you?

B   Yes, could I speak to Mr Travers?

A   Yes, I'll try and [1] **put**/*connect* you through. May I ask who's [2] *calling/talking*?

B   Yes, [3] *this is/here is* Paul Hunter.

A   I'm afraid that extension is [4] *occupied/busy*. Would you like to [5] *hold/stay*?

B   Yes, that's fine.

A   It's [6] *ringing/calling* for you now.

C   Hello, Reservations. Jenny Rathbone [7] *talking/speaking*. Can I help you?

B   Yes, is Mr Travers there, please?

C   No, I'm [8] *regret/afraid* he's out at the moment. Would you like to [9] *give/leave* a message?

B   Yes, could you ask him to call Paul Hunter as soon as possible?

C   I'm sorry, I didn't [10] *catch/have* that. This is rather a bad [11] *line/extension*. Could you [12] *relate/repeat* that?

B   Yes, could you tell him that Paul Hunter rang and ask him to [13] *call/get* back to me as soon as possible. He [14] *has/holds* my number.

C   OK. I'll make sure he [15] *gets/listens* the message. Goodbye.

B   Goodbye.

Read the following information and answer the questions below.

3

Travel agents

About the FREEway programme

Welcome to **Virgin** FREEway, Virgin Atlantic's frequent flyer programme. As a FREEway member you can earn valuable FREEway miles when flying with Virgin Atlantic or using services of our partner companies.

You can redeem your miles for flights, hotel accommodation, car hire, holiday vouchers and a whole range of leisure activities, ranging from a parachuting lesson to a luxury holiday on Necker Island, Richard Branson's exclusive Caribbean island.

About the FREEway benefits

Virgin FREEway is Virgin Atlantic's frequent flyer programme designed especially for Upper Class and Premium Economy travellers resident in the UK, US, Japan, Hong Kong, Southern Africa, and Greece.

All you need do to become a member is to ask cabin staff for a FREEway enrolment form when you next fly on Virgin Atlantic, fill it in and return it to Virgin Atlantic. Or call us on **0171 924 9105**.

FREEway benefits

For your first Upper Class round trip as a FREEway member you'll earn enough miles for two Economy round trip flights from London to Europe.

* Double miles flown on all Upper Class flights
* Enough miles for a free Economy ticket from London to Europe after each Upper Class return flight
* Mile for mile in Premium Economy
* Mile for mile in Economy after qualifying flights
* Partners such as British Midland, SAS, Austrian Airlines, Air New Zealand, Avis, Forte, Texaco (UK only), American Express, Inter-Continental Hotels, Radisson SAS Hotels Worldwide, Summit International Hotels, Holiday Inn (UK only), Virgin Hotels, Le Manoir aux Quat' Saisons, Westin, Mandarin Oriental
* Travel rewards including free hotel accommodation, car rental and holiday vouchers
* Activity rewards including tandem skydiving, hot-air ballooning and off-road driving

BOOKING YOUR REWARDS

To book your reward, simply call the FREEway helpline on **0171 924 9105** between 09.00 and 17.00 Monday to Friday. All rewards are strictly subject to availability.

Make sure you book your reward at least twenty-one days, and no more than ten months, prior to departure. If you request a reward between twenty and seven days prior to departure you will incur an express handling fee of GRD 9,300 per transaction. Please remember no reward request can be accepted within seven days of departure.

Once issued, unused tickets/vouchers may be changed for a handling fee of GRD 9,300. (Please note, no changes may be made to Delta or Eurostar tickets.)

If you cancel a reward ticket/voucher you can have 75% of your miles recredited to your FREEway account, providing you notify **Virgin** FREEway of any cancellations at least seven days before departure. This will incur a handling fee of GRD 9,300 per ticket/voucher.

As a FREEway member you can redeem your miles to obtain a reward for anyone of your choice. You are the only one who can authorize this reward and once a third party reward is issued, it is not transferable.

To request a FREEway statement or balance enquiry, call faxfile on **01293 538888** from any phone in the UK. This response will be sent instantly to any fax in the UK.

Virgin FREEway

Are the following statements true (T) or false (F)?

1 You do not have to fly Virgin Atlantic to earn Freeway miles.
2 You can use your Freeway miles to buy a vacation on a private Caribbean island.
3 Residents of the US are not allowed to take part in the scheme.
4 You can apply to join the scheme when you are on a Virgin Atlantic flight.
5 You must fly in Upper Class or Premium Economy to start earning miles now.
6 You can earn extra miles if you stay at a Holiday Inn when in the US.
7 To book a reward, you must ring during office hours.
8 You must give at least one week's notice to book a reward.
9 You have to pay a small charge to change a reward that you have booked.
10 You don't have to use a reward yourself – you can give it to someone else.

Dialogue completion

A business customer has asked you for some information about Virgin's frequent flyer programme. Complete the dialogue using the information in exercise 7, but use your own words as much as possible. The first one has been done for you.

CUSTOMER I was talking to a colleague in the office the other day and he mentioned it might be an idea to join Freeway – do you know anything about it?

AGENT 1 *Yes, it's an air miles scheme run by Virgin, and you collect points or air miles every time you fly, and you can use them to get free flights depending on how many air miles you've collected.*

CUSTOMER I see, but presumably you can only get these air miles if you fly with Virgin?

AGENT 2 _____

CUSTOMER That's better. And what sort of things can you use them for?

AGENT 3 _____

CUSTOMER What about if I went to, say New York, for a holiday with my family? We'd probably go economy, but could I put all the air miles on my account?

AGENT 4 _____

CUSTOMER Oh, I thought there had to be a catch. So what would I get, for example, if I flew to the States on my own on business and went Upper Class?

AGENT 5 _____

CUSTOMER Ah, that sounds better. Tell me, is there any other way of getting air miles – or can you basically only get them by flying?

AGENT 6 _____

CUSTOMER OK, now what about booking. Let's say I had enough miles for a trip to Paris, could I just turn up at the airport and buy a ticket?

AGENT 7 _____

CUSTOMER I see. Just one more thing – what would happen if I wanted to, you know, give someone a flight to Paris as a present – my daughter, for example? Would it be OK for her to get a ticket even though they're my air miles?

AGENT 8 _____

CUSTOMER Yes, all right then. Have you got a form I can fill in or something?

AGENT 9 _____

CUSTOMER Thank you very much.

4

Tour operation

1   Travel agents and tour operators

A Look though the following extracts from letters, memos, e-mails, and faxes. Decide whether they were written by (a) a travel agent or (b) a tour operator. The first one has been done for you.

1 __d__   *As I mentioned to you on the phone, we are confident that there will be more firm bookings for you soon. In the meantime, could you send us another 500 Summer Sun brochures, as we are running low on stock?*

2 ___   Enclosed is the rooming list for the group arriving on 18 August. Please note that there have been some last minute cancellations, and we now only require thirty-five double rooms.

3 ___   Dear Mr Smith,
I enclose your tickets to Los Angeles for 11 May and am also sending two vouchers to cover the cost of accommodation at the Holiday Inn.
I hope you have a pleasant trip.
Yours sincerely,
Jean Hayward

4 ——   We will be discussing the discount you have offered for bulk purchase of seats during our next managerial meeting, and I hope to get back to you with our response by Friday at the latest.

5 ——   *As yet we have not drawn up a contract for the bulk purchase of rooms from Orion Hotel Group for next year. Please arrange a meeting with Mr Killick so that I can discuss the matter with him.*

6 ——   One of the matters that I will raise at the meeting is the organization of racks, as there have been several complaints from customers that these are confusing.

7 ——   As a result of the fire, two of the units in the Elina Apartments have been damaged and will almost certainly not be available. I am currently negotiating with the owner of a similar property nearby, and will contact you as soon as I have any firm information.

8 ——   Further to the flight manifest I faxed to you this morning, I enclose details of passengers who have requested vegetarian meals.

B Complete the wordsquare by filling in the missing words in the sentences below. All the words have appeared in the extracts you have just read. The first one has been done for you.

1					C	o	n	t	r	a	c	t
2												
3												
4												
5												
6												
7												
8												

1 A ___ is a legal agreement between two people or companies. (8)

2 A flight ___ contains the names of passengers who are on a particular flight. (8)

3 In most travel agencies, leaflets and other travel information is displayed on ___ . (5)

4 A ___ list gives details of all the people who have been booked into a hotel. (7)

5 A ___ is a reduction in price that is usually given for bulk purchases. (8)

6 ___ is the process of discussing terms and conditions and trying to come to an agreement. (11)

7 A ___ is a piece of paper that can be exchanged for something like food or accommodation. (7)

8 ___ are publicity booklets produced by tour operator which give details of the holidays they offer. (9)

Types of message

A Below is a series of different types of message (e-mail, letter, fax, telephone message) exchanged between a tour operator, a supplier, and a travel agent. Some of the sentences have been removed. Read the texts and then look at **B**.

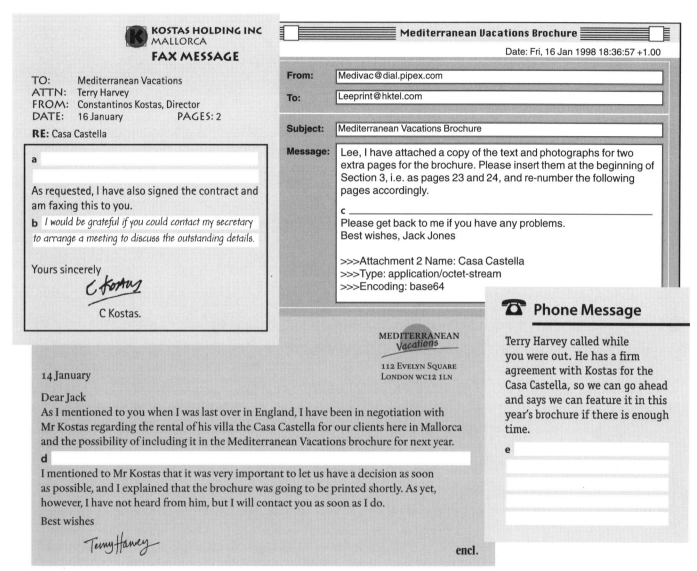

K KOSTAS HOLDING INC
MALLORCA

FAX MESSAGE

TO: Mediterranean Vacations
ATTN: Terry Harvey
FROM: Constantinos Kostas, Director
DATE: 16 January   PAGES: 2

RE: Casa Castella

a _____

As requested, I have also signed the contract and am faxing this to you.

b *I would be grateful if you could contact my secretary to arrange a meeting to discuss the outstanding details.*

Yours sincerely

C Kostas

C Kostas.

Mediterranean Vacations Brochure

Date: Fri, 16 Jan 1998 18:36:57 +1.00

From: Medivac@dial.pipex.com

To: Leeprint@hktel.com

Subject: Mediterranean Vacations Brochure

Message: Lee, I have attached a copy of the text and photographs for two extra pages for the brochure. Please insert them at the beginning of Section 3, i.e. as pages 23 and 24, and re-number the following pages accordingly.

c _____
Please get back to me if you have any problems.
Best wishes, Jack Jones

>>>Attachment 2 Name: Casa Castella
>>>Type: application/octet-stream
>>>Encoding: base64

☎ **Phone Message**

Terry Harvey called while you were out. He has a firm agreement with Kostas for the Casa Castella, so we can go ahead and says we can feature it in this year's brochure if there is enough time.

e _____
_____
_____

MEDITERRANEAN *Vacations*

112 EVELYN SQUARE
LONDON WC12 1LN

14 January

Dear Jack

As I mentioned to you when I was last over in England, I have been in negotiation with Mr Kostas regarding the rental of his villa the Casa Castella for our clients here in Mallorca and the possibility of including it in the Mediterranean Vacations brochure for next year.

d _____

I mentioned to Mr Kostas that it was very important to let us have a decision as soon as possible, and I explained that the brochure was going to be printed shortly. As yet, however, I have not heard from him, but I will contact you as soon as I do.

Best wishes

Terry Harvey

encl.

B The following sentences have been removed from the messages above. Read through the texts again and put the missing sentences in the correct place. The first one has been done for you.

1 *I would be grateful if you could contact my secretary to arrange a meeting to discuss the outstanding details.*

2 I apologize for this late change, but it was due to circumstances beyond our control.

3 I have enclosed photographs of the property and a description of the villa and the area. As you will see, it is very desirable, and as it has six bedrooms and a swimming pool, I believe it would be very popular if we could include it. I have offered him fairly favourable terms because I believe that he has approached a number of other local tour operators with a view to renting it out.

4 He says you can ring him back if there's anything else you need to know – he'll be in the office most of this afternoon.

5 I am pleased to inform you that I have decided to accept your terms for the rental of the Casa Castella for the next two years.

C Work out the order in which the various messages were sent and complete the table below. The first one has been done for you.

1 The first message was the ___letter___ from _____ to _____.

2 The second message was the _____ from _____ to _____.

3 The third message was the _____ from _____ to _____.

4 The fourth message was the _____ from _____ to _____.

3   Setting up negotiations

Read the following dialogue. Choose the correct option from the words in italics. The first one has been done for you.

MICHAEL   Hello, Jeanette, this is Michael from Spanish Steps. How are things going with you?

JEANETTE   Oh, very well. We're quite busy because we've just taken delivery of some new coaches.

MICHAEL   Oh, right, well, in fact that is what I was ringing about. I thought we [1] **ought to**/*must* get together and discuss the arrangements for next year.

JEANETTE   Yes, that sounds like a good [2] *idea/possibility*. What [3] *about/for* Wednesday 30th?

MICHAEL   No, that's not very [4] *available/convenient* for me. I [5] *could/shall* do the Thursday – can you?

JEANETTE   Yes, that looks good. Shall we [6] *arrange/say* 2.30?

MICHAEL   Yes, that would be fine.

JEANETTE   Is there anything in particular that you'd like to [7] *bring/take* up?

MICHAEL   Yes, I thought it [8] *might/can* be useful to talk about how many clients we'll be sending over and how many coaches we'll be likely to need.

JEANETTE   Yes, I [9] *agree/am agreed*. Perhaps we could talk about prices as well. Obviously we've made a big capital investment, and we're going to need a little extra to reflect the money we've spent.

MICHAEL   Well, I [10] *understand/interpret* what you're saying, but perhaps we can look at other ways of making sure you get extra revenue.

JEANETTE   OK, well, we can look at that. Was there [11] *other things/anything else*?

MICHAEL   Yes, there was one other thing. I'd like to bring up the matter of reliability – we had quite a lot of complaints about late departures, and we felt we got a bit of a raw deal to be [12] *honest/true*.

JEANETTE   Well, maybe, but I'm sure that things will be better now. Is that everything?

MICHAEL   Yes, I think so – we've got a pretty full agenda there. I [13] *look forward to/am happy* seeing you again.

JEANETTE   OK, I'll see you at 2.30 on the 31st. Goodbye.

Preliminary negotiations

Read the following situations. Using your own ideas, write down what you might say.

1 You are on the phone with a client whose hotels you use for your tours. He has just suggested meeting next Wednesday, but you would prefer to meet on Friday at 11.00.

CLIENT What about meeting next week – say Wednesday at 2.30?

YOU _____

_____

2 Your client asks if there is anything in particular you want to talk about. You want to discuss how many rooms you will need for next season. You also want a price reduction, but don't want to go into details now.

CLIENT Is there anything in particular that you'd like to bring up?

YOU _____

_____

3 Your client wants to discuss the complaints you had last year. You think this is a good idea, and suggest bringing along some of the letters you have received from dissatisfied customers.

CLIENT Perhaps we could look at any complaints you had last year and see if there are any problems we can sort out.

YOU _____

_____

4 Your client suggests that he may have to raise prices; this is absolutely unacceptable. Say you understand his point, but might consider booking more rooms instead.

CLIENT Now, as I am sure you know, the changes in the exchange rate mean that there will have to be to a modest increase in our charges, or we'll end up losing money.

YOU _____

_____

5 Your client asks if there is anything else to discuss; your directors have insisted that you talk about the high cancellation charges, which they felt were unreasonable.

CLIENT Is there anything else that you'd like on the agenda?

YOU _____

_____

6 You have decided to bring the phone call to a close. Finish by confirming the time of your meeting.

CLIENT I'll make sure that the meeting room is free, and I'll bring along the documents I mentioned.

YOU _____

_____

Responding to complaints

Read the following complaints and responses. Then complete the exercises below.

Complaints

Responses

a
We still haven't received confirmation that the coach has been booked, and this is the fifth time that I've rung you.

b
I'm just calling to say that the brochures haven't arrived – do you think you could send us some more because we're running quite low?

1
Oh why don't you just stop moaning and leave me alone.

2
I'm sorry about that. I'll have a look at the file and see what I can find out.

c
It's really much too hot for me here. I think we should have been warned, you know, and another thing, I saw those Jones children in the pool yesterday, and they were very noisy, and then last night I was bitten by a mosquito. We're not going to come on holiday with you again, you know.

3
I'm sorry but there isn't anything I can do. The flight is fully booked, and there just aren't any free seats available.

4
Yes, of course – I'm very sorry. I'll make sure you get another hundred by Friday.

d
Look, we are not going to move into a room without a sea view. The brochure clearly stated that we would be given one and we paid extra for it, and we're going to sit here in reception until you sort it out.

e
Surely you can't expect us to have the baby on our lap for the whole flight?

5
I'm terribly sorry, you're absolutely right. I'll go and see the manager immediately and get you moved. I know there are still a few ones free, so you needn't worry.

A Match the complaints with the responses. The first one has been done for you.

a _2_   b ___   c ___   d ___   e ___

B Now put the responses in order. Which were the most helpful, and which were the least helpful?

Most helpful   *Least helpful*

___   ___   ___   ___   ___

C Using your own ideas, reply to the following complaints by holidaymakers on one of your tours. Try to be as helpful as possible.

1 My wife has been very ill for the last two days. I really don't know what to do.

_____

2 I'm afraid our holiday has got off to a rather bad start. The noise from the road is really terrible, and I find it quite hard to sleep.

_____

3 I find it hard to believe that here we are at the start of the summer season and the swimming pool is empty.

_____

4 We did say that we wanted to hire a Suzuki jeep, not a Fiat Cinquecento. Do you think you can sort it out?

_____

5 I'm afraid I can't eat this hotel food any more. If I see another Greek salad, I think I'll be sick.

_____

Read the following letter from a tour operator to a customer and complete the exercises that follow.

◆ **VillageVillas**

22 Bakers Lane
Bristol BS10 5JJ

t: 0117 067678
f: 0117 067855
e: info@villvilla.com

30 September

Dear Mrs Lewis,

Thank you for your letter of 18 September. *I was sorry to hear* that you were disappointed by the service you received on your holiday.

I have investigated your complaint that the villa was not cleaned by the maid on the last two days of your holiday. I have spoken to our representative in Corfu, and it seems that *the problems were due to* the fact that the maid was ill. *Unfortunately,* we were not able to find a replacement at such short notice.

Please accept my sincere apologies. I can assure you that we will take steps to ensure that this does not occur again. As a sign of goodwill, I enclose a brochure for next year and a voucher which entitles you to 10% off the advertised price of any holiday booked before 31 January.

Yours sincerely,

P Merson

P Merson
Customer Services Manager

A Are the following statements true (T) or false (F)?

1 Mrs Lewis has phoned the company to complain.
2 Mrs Lewis had a problem with the maid at the villa.
3 The representative in Corfu made some attempt to solve the problem.
4 The company was entirely responsible for what went wrong.
5 The manager says he has taken action to stop the problem from happening again.
6 The manager offers the customer a small refund.

B Write a short letter of apology based on the notes below, which you have received from a colleague. Try and use the words in italics from the sample letter in your answer.

We've received a complaint from Judy Elson, passenger on flight BR 354 to Mallorca. Ordered a vegetarian meal, but didn't get one. Have looked into this – problem was that the van with the veggie meals broke down on the way to the airport. Please draft reply, send apologies, etc.

_____
_____
_____
_____
_____
_____
_____
_____

5

Air travel

1 Vocabulary

At the airport

A travel agent is explaining what to do at the airport to a customer who has not travelled by plane before. Complete the sentences with one word from column **A** and one word from column **B**. The first one has been done for you.

A	B
conveyor	desk
departure	card
terminal	class
hand	lounge
check-in	baggage
economy	*building*
departure	control
excess	luggage
boarding	belt
passport	gate

Most taxi drivers know the airport quite well, so if you tell him where you are going, he'll drop you off at the right [1] _terminal_ _building_. When you get inside, go to the [2] _____ _____ and have your ticket and passport ready. As you're travelling [3] _____ _____, the queues can be quite long, so make sure you get there in good time. You'll be given your [4] _____ _____ with your seat number, and they'll weigh your bags, which will then get taken away on a [5] _____ _____. You can carry one item of [6] _____ _____ with you onto the plane, but if your cases weigh more than 20 kgs, you'll have to pay [7] _____ _____, which can be very expensive. Just before you go into the [8] _____ _____, you'll have to go through [9] _____ _____ or a final check, and then listen out for the announcement to tell you which [10] _____ _____ you need to go to in order to board the plane.

Talking about procedures

A A participant on a cabin crew training course has been asked to repeat the safety procedure for passengers during an emergency landing at sea. Read the passage and choose the best word or phrase from the options a–c. The first one has been done for you.

¹ *First of all* you have to make an announcement explaining that there will be an emergency landing, and ² _____ afterwards you need to keep the passengers calm, because you want to avoid panic. ³ _____ as this, you make sure that they put out any cigarettes and get into the emergency landing position, with their heads down. ⁴ _____ before landing is for the members of the crew to get into the emergency landing position as well. ⁵ _____ the plane has landed, you open the emergency doors, let down the escape chute and send down a member of the cabin crew to inflate the life-raft. ⁶ _____ you begin to evacuate the passengers, making sure that they have removed high-heeled shoes and have put on their life-jackets ⁷ _____. You tell them to go down the chute and to inflate their life-jackets ⁸ _____, and to head for the life-raft. ⁹ _____ is to check that all the passengers have escaped and ¹⁰ _____ you leave the plane yourself.

1 a beforehand	b *first of all*	c previously
2 a immediately	b previously	c finally
3 a simultaneously	b at the same time	c while
4 a finally	b the last stage	c prior to this
5 a on	b as soon as	c soon
6 a previously	b then	c after
7 a immediately afterwards	b simultaneously	c beforehand
8 a while	b simultaneously	c previously
9 a next	b the last stage	c immediately afterwards
10 a finally	b prior to this	c beforehand

B Write a short paragraph explaining what the cabin crew need to do between the time the passengers arrive on a plane and the time the first drinks are served. Use some of the linking words above and the following notes.

a greet passengers
b show passengers to seats
c check numbers
d make safety announcement
e check seat-belts are fastened, seats are upright, and luggage in overhead lockers
f check that emergency exits are clear
g take seats for take-off
h make in-flight announcement
i serve drinks

_____
_____
_____
_____

3 Vocabulary — Air travel

A Put the words in the box into the correct areas of the word map. The first one has been done for you.

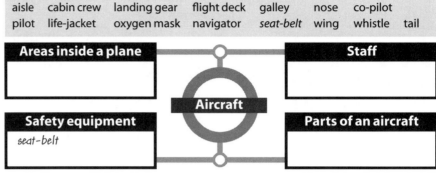

| aisle | cabin crew | landing gear | flight deck | galley | nose | co-pilot |
| pilot | life-jacket | oxygen mask | navigator | *seat-belt* | wing | whistle | tail |

Areas inside a plane

Staff

Aircraft

Safety equipment
seat-belt

Parts of an aircraft

B Think of four things you might say to a passenger during a flight or in an announcement. Use at least one of the words above in each sentence. The first has been done for you.

1 *Would Mr Fukiyama please make himself known to a member of the cabin crew.*

2 _____

3 _____

4 _____

4 Writing — Seating arrangements

◄ Mary Watson, 45, journalist.

▼ Jack Winters, 34, businessman.

▼ Mr and Mrs Jones and their six-month-old baby.

◄ Helen Hamblin, 44, journalist and colleague of Mary Watson.

Anna Mason, 11, ► who is travelling alone.

A A temporary check-in clerk has not allocated the passengers' seats correctly, and you have received a number of complaints. Read the complaints and the information, and re-allocate the seats so that everyone is happy.

STEWARD	You can't have an infant in the second row– the cots are all at the front. And another thing, you can't seat an unaccompanied minor next to a man.
MARY WATSON	Couldn't I sit next to Ms Hamblin – we've got work to discuss.
JACK WINTERS	I asked for a window seat, and I don't think I could stand being anywhere near that baby.
MR AND MRS JONES	Surely it must be possible for us to be seated together?
HELEN HAMBLIN	I don't know why you want to change everything. I'm happy with my aisle seat and don't see why I should move.
ANNA MASON	Please don't take my window seat away.

Original seating plan

	window	centre	aisle
Row 1	Mary Watson	Mr Jones	Helen Hamblin
Row 2	Anna Mason	Jack Winters	Mrs Jones + infant

Improved seating plan

	window	centre	aisle
Row 1			
Row 2			

B Write a short paragraph explaining why you have chosen this arrangement.

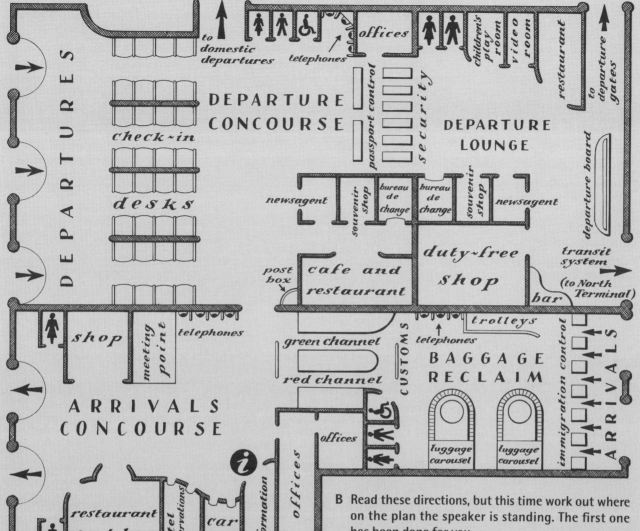

A Look at the plan of the terminal building of a modern airport. Read the directions and work out where the passenger is going. The first one has been done for you.

1 After you get through customs go straight on and it's ahead of you, just to the right, next to the phones. You can't miss it – there's a big sign.
meeting point

2 There's one over there where the shops are, third shop on the left, opposite the café. There's another one in the departure lounge: go straight ahead and once you're through passport control and security it's immediately on your right.

_____

3 Go in through the revolving doors, past the check-in desks, and it's over in the right-hand corner, next to the restaurant.

_____

B Read these directions, but this time work out where on the plan the speaker is standing. The first one has been done for you.

1 Go out of the door and turn left and left again and the toilets are over on your right, just next to the security desk.
duty-free shop

2 Go diagonally left and there's a ladies' just round to the left of the shop. The men's is opposite if you want.

_____

3 Just go along here past the other shops towards the departures board then turn right and you'll see the duty-free shop. The bar's just a bit further on, right at the very end of the departure lounge.

_____

C Now give directions to the following passengers.

1 Mrs Jones is in the souvenir shop, and is about to go to the departure lounge. She wants to know where to find the children's play room.

2 Mr Watson is in the baggage reclaim area and wants to know where to find the car-hire desk.

You are in charge of membership of the International Executive Lounge Club. You have received a message on the answerphone from Mr Robert Klein, Manager of TKL Enterprises, 86 March Street, London SW1, enquiring about your services and charges. He travels extensively, and recently heard about the club from a colleague, but does not have any of the details. Read through the leaflet and write a suitable reply.

THE INTERNATIONAL EXECUTIVE LOUNGE CLUB
Now operating at over 80 major international airports worldwide

Recently opened, the International Executive Lounge Club provides international business travellers with private surroundings at over eighty airports world-wide. Becoming a member will provide you with a space where you can relax or catch up with work before boarding your flight or when you are in transit.

Members of the club are entitled to the following benefits in any of our Lounges:

- complimentary tea and coffee
- bar, snack bar and restaurant (*restrictions apply to the sale of alcohol in certain countries*)

In addition, we provide a full range of facilities to meet the needs of business travellers:

- secretarial / dictating services
- fax machines and photocopiers
- personal computers and Internet connections
- meeting rooms and small offices (Cost: US$20 per hour, *subject to availability*)

Other facilities include:

- local and international TV
- full range of newspapers and magazines
- comfortable seating area
- complimentary shower and toilet facilities

Annual membership of the Executive Club Lounge International costs just US$180, and members are entitled to make unlimited use of the facilities in any country.

For instant membership using your credit card, please contact us on
(UK) **0181 232 8833**:
Visa/American Express/Mastercard/Diners Club

Alternatively, please write to us at:
IELC
Airways House
236 Southern Avenue
London W11 3HT.

Notes on answering a letter of enquiry

1 Layout
Make sure that you lay out your letter correctly. You will be using headed writing paper, so you do not need to write your address. You should write Mr Klein's address (86 March Street, London SW1) and the date in the correct position.

2 Beginning
Begin your letter with a reference to his enquiry. Useful phrases:
I am writing in response to …   Thank you for your enquiry about …
I would like to tell you about …

3 Facilities
Give the customer an idea of the main facilities that you offer. You can divide this up into three sections: facilities related to relaxing, facilities related to carrying out business, facilities related to washing and cleaning.

4 Prices
Give the customer an indication of prices. In this section give information about some of the prices. Give details of the cost of the lounge area and what it includes and give details of the cost of work stations. Useful phrases:
Our prices are extremely competitive.
In addition …
Not only does this include … but it also includes …

5 Ending
Finish your letter with a suitable ending. For example:
Should you require any further information please do not hesitate to contact me.
I look forward to hearing from you.

Read the following newspaper article. Say if the statements below are true (T) or false (F) according to the text.

Want to join the JET SET?

Just thinking about being a member of the cabin crew should be enough to put you off. The scene is just after take-off – you're working in a space not much bigger than a caravan and have hundreds of meals to serve. Babies are screaming, nervous flyers are calling for your attention, and a couple of the passengers who have had too much to drink are already being aggressive. On top of that, you have disgruntled non-smokers in the smoking section who are demanding to be re-seated.

That's what it's like on a good day, and it can get a lot worse. Despite security improvements, there is still the possibility of being hijacked or having a bomb on board, and there is a constant risk of a crash.

Even so, there is no shortage of people who want what many people think of as one of the most glamorous jobs in the travel industry. After all, even if there is a downside, you get the chance to see the world and someone else will pick up the bill. You stay in great hotels, never see the inside of an office, and think nothing of spending the weekend in Australia.

Given that the job has its attractions, what are the airlines looking for? Most people still believe that you need the face and figure of a model, but the airlines say this is not the case. Certainly there are some requirements – you need to be between 19 and 35, and to be at least 1m 57 tall. You'll need to look smart and to be prepared to conform to the airline's dress code, which is usually conservative.

Apart from that, you'll need to convince them that you will be able to perform the major role of a cabin crew member, which is to look after the safety needs of the passengers. That means staying calm in a crisis and being able to manage difficult situations before they get out of hand. You don't need a university degree, but a knowledge of languages is obviously useful. It helps if you are reasonably numerate and you'll need to be able to swim.

If you do get through the interview, you'll be sent on a training course, which will last for a month or perhaps a couple of weeks longer, and your first job might bring you about £12,000 p.a. Job satisfaction will depend on what kind of airline you are working for. If you're going backwards and forwards on charter flights, you may just spend most of your time inside the plane or a terminal building. Long haul flights are more fun. You'll have the chance to have longer breaks of three or four days at a time at more exotic destinations. Of course it will play havoc with your social life, but as you sun yourself on a sandy Caribbean beach while everyone else you know is battling through the rush hour in the rain and snow, you'll probably find that you won't mind too much.

1 The writer suggests that working as a member of the cabin crew is fairly easy.
2 Because of security problems, cabin crew jobs have become more dangerous.
3 The airlines are finding it difficult to recruit cabin crew staff.
4 The main advantage of the job is that your travel costs are paid.
5 You do not need to be attractive to become a flight attendant.
6 Airlines are interested in standards of personal appearance.
7 Airlines prefer cabin crew to be educated to degree level.
8 Most training courses last at least a month.
9 Short-haul flights are less satisfying than long-haul flights.
10 Most cabin crew members start on charter flights.

6

Travel by sea and river – cruises and ferries

1 Reading

Information about a cruise

A The following text gives information to passengers going on a cruise. Some of the sentences have been removed. Read the text and then look at **B**.

Your holiday questions answered

○ **Can my friends come and see me off?**
• Of course your friends are welcome to give you the traditional send-off from the pier side. 1 _____

○ **When do I eat?**
• There are two sittings for meals and you can request the sitting you'd prefer, the table size you'd like. Where there is particularly heavy demand for one sitting, tables will be allocated in order of booking date. 2 _____

○ **Special diets.**
• Naturally we can provide diabetic, fat-free, vegetarian, and gluten-free meals. 3 _____ In order to give us plenty of time to place the necessary orders and to give you the best possible service, please let us know your needs three to four weeks in advance.

○ **Talking of children ...**
• We want your whole family to have a wonderful holiday and we therefore provide a daily programme for children. 4 _____ For children aged two to nine, all four ships have a Junior Club which is open from 9 a.m. to 10 p.m. 5 _____ This operates from 6 p.m. to 2 a.m. and on *Oriana*, there is an in-cabin baby listening facility.

○ **I love to shop. Can you help?**
• As you'd expect, your sea-going home can provide all sorts of necessities you may have forgotten to bring – toothpaste, batteries, film, chocolate, postcards. What you may not expect, however, is the dazzling array of luxury items. 6 _____

○ **What about keeping healthy?**
• Quite apart from our programmes of exercise and keep-fit classes, you'll find we have ample facilities for those who wish to stay in shape. Another reassuring fact is that all our ships have a fully equipped medical centre, complete with doctors and nurses. 7 _____

○ **What about a good read?**
• All ships have a library where you'll find a good selection of books, both fact and fiction. 8 _____

○ **Money matters.**
• For your convenience, P&O operates a cash-free system on board. 9 _____

○ **Going ashore**
• Wherever possible, your ship will dock, allowing you to come and go as you please. Sometimes, in smaller ports, the ship will anchor at sea. 10 _____ While the ship is in port, the restaurants, bars and other facilities will be available to you.

○ **To tour or not to tour?**
• It's your decision entirely. We offer a comprehensive range of full- and half-day tours at most ports. We will send you full details about six weeks before you sail. 11 *Sentence a* If you prefer to make your own arrangements, you'll find a folder of port guides in your cabin.

B The sentences below have been removed from the text. Read the text again and put them into the correct places. The first one has been done for you.

a *Advance booking is recommended, though naturally you can book at the tours office on board.*

b And every day a copy of the ship's newspaper will be delivered to your cabin to keep you up to date with all the activities on board.

c Treatment is charged at private rates, but you'll find that in most cases you will be covered by your holiday insurance.

d But for security reasons, visitors are not permitted on board *Arcadia, Canberra, Victoria,* or *Oriana,* or in the passenger terminal.

e All your purchases can be signed for and your account can be settled by credit card, charge card, or cash at the end of your cruise.

f Fine perfumes, cameras, personal stereos, and evening wear can all be bought on board at tempting shipboard prices.

g Kosher food can also be provided.

h Please remember that tables for two are extremely limited and cannot be guaranteed.

i At the start of your holiday you'll be invited to an informal meeting where our Youth Staff will explain the facilities in detail.

j In this case, a free shuttle service ashore will be provided.

k Children under five can also be left in our supervised night nursery.

2   Passive tense review

A You have been asked to write the 'welcome aboard' notice for passengers at the beginning of a cruise on the *Ramada Diamond.* Complete the paragraphs below using the notes and the tenses indicated. The first one has been done for you in each case.

a **present perfect (active or passive)**
ship/completely modernize
The ship has been completely modernized.
the restaurants/extensively redecorate
fitness centre/open/Deck C
we/also/build/new pool/upper deck

b **simple present (active or passive)**
breakfast/serve daily/from 7–11
Breakfast is served daily from 7–11.
The main restaurants/open/at midday/close/12.30
We/offer/24-hour room service
Please note/small charge/make/for this

c ***will* future (active or passive)**
You/have the chance/go ashore/shopping or sightseeing
You will have the chance to go ashore for shopping or sightseeing.
Passengers/take/to the port/by speedboat
You/collect/ 6.30 p.m.
we/set sail again at 9.00 p.m.

d **simple past (active or passive)**
one of the passengers/get /hold up /during a shore visit
One of the passengers got held up during a shore visit.
As a result/he/leave behind
we/have to/set sail/without him
fortunately/he/pick up/next port of call

B Now use the paragraphs you have written above to complete the text of the 'welcome aboard' notice.

Welcome aboard

1 Ladies and gentlemen, welcome aboard the *Ramada Diamond* and to our cruise of the Caribbean. If you have sailed with us before, you will notice that the ship
has been completely modernized.
_____
_____

2 We sincerely hope that you will enjoy the gourmet food we provide and would like to remind you of mealtimes in the main restaurants …
_____
_____
_____

3 Our first port of call will be St Lucia on Wednesday.
_____
_____
_____

4 Please note: may we remind you of the importance of pick-up times, as there was an unfortunate incident on one of our recent cruises.
_____
_____
_____

We trust that this will not happen to you and hope you have an enjoyable cruise.

C A tour operator is talking to a colleague about a disastrous cruise. Read what he says and rewrite the information using the passive in the appropriate tense. The first one has been done for you.

'It's been terrible. Apparently, yesterday, at the start of the cruise they were still redecorating the ship – and in fact the last I heard was that they are still painting the cabins and have only opened one of the restaurants. Everyone is furious with the company, but you can't blame them – they couldn't delay the start of the cruise because the contractors hadn't told them about the problems. I think our clients will be OK because they usually compensate passengers for this sort of thing, but they'll definitely fine the company.'

1 The ship/redecorate
The ship was still being redecorated.
_____

2 The cabins/still/paint
_____

3 Only one of the restaurants/open
_____

4 The start of the cruise/not delay
_____

5 They/tell/about the problems
_____

6 Passengers/compensate/this sort of thing
_____

7 The company/definitely/fine
_____

3   Issuing tickets

Read the following dialogue. Choose the correct option from the words in italics. The first one has been done for you.

CUSTOMER	Could you give me [1] **some**/an information about boats to Paxos?
CLERK	Yes, when would you like to go?
CUSTOMER	[2] *After tomorrow/The day after tomorrow.*
CLERK	There's a hydrofoil – the Pegasus, which leaves at 11.30 every day [3] *except/apart* Sunday. It gets [4] *in/to* Paxos at 2.30, and stops at Lakka and Gaios.
CUSTOMER	How much [5] *are/cost* the tickets?
CLERK	An adult [6] *fare/fee* is 5,000 drachmas.
CUSTOMER	Is that [7] *one-way/single* or return?
CLERK	Return.
CUSTOMER	And is there any reduction for children?
CLERK	Yes there's a discount of 50% for children from five to sixteen, and under-fives are free.
CUSTOMER	Do you have to book in [8] *ahead/advance*?
CLERK	No, you can get tickets on [9] *board/ship*.
CUSTOMER	How long is the journey?
CLERK	It depends a bit on the weather, but it usually [10] *needs/takes* two and a half hours.

4   Forms of the future

A *Will* or present simple?
Read the following sentences. In each sentence, put one of the verbs into the *will* future and the other into the present simple.

1 I _____ (give) you a ring as soon as the tickets _____ (arrive).

2 A motor launch _____ (take) passengers ashore when the ship _____ (arrive) at Grenada.

3 I _____ (give) your message to the captain before he _____ (leave).

4 I _____ (contact) you before I _____ (confirm) the booking.

5 When we _____ (get) to Luxor, we _____ (visit) the temple of Karnak.

B *Will* or *going to*?
Fill in the blanks with *will* or the correct form of *going to*.

1 a Have you organized your summer holiday yet?

   b Yes, we _____ go on a cruise round the Greek Islands.

2 a Do you know if there are still any places on the excursion to Abu Simbel?

   b I'm not sure – I _____ have a word with the purser and let you know.

3 a I _____ get another film from the shop. Do you need anything?

   b No thanks. See you later.

4 a What do you need your passport for?

   b I _____ change some traveller's cheques.

5 a I'm a bit worried about leaving these valuables in the cabin.

   b Of course, madam. We _____ keep them for you in the safe if you like.

C Itineraries

One of your customers has booked a cruise to St Vincent and the Grenadines on board a luxury charter yacht. Give your customer details of the cruise based on the following information. The first one has been done for you.

▶	**Monday**	Arrive in St Vincent spend half a day in St Vincent set sail at 6.00 p.m.
	Tuesday	Travel to Bequia afternoon visit to whaling museum
	Wednesday	Spend in Mustique lunch at Charleston Bay
	Thursday	Go to Palm Island chance to go scuba diving
	Friday	Cross to Union Island catch 06.25 connecting flight to St Lucia overnight at St Lucia Paradise Hotel
	Saturday	Fly back to London ETA 18.30 local time

You're arriving in St Vincent on Monday; you're spending the day there and the yacht sets sail at 6.00 in the evening. On Tuesday, _____

_____

_____

_____

_____

5 International etiquette

Look at these examples of advice for visitors to Britain.

Be careful to tip taxi drivers about ten per cent, as they can be offended if you only offer them the fare shown on the meter.

If you are invited to a British person's home for dinner, make sure you arrive a few minutes late.

Think of similar examples of advice for foreigners coming to your country. Use some of the expressions in the box:

It's a good idea (not) to	Make sure you (don't)	If possible, visitors should(n't)
Never .../ Always ...	Take care you don't ...	Be careful (not) to ...

1 _____

2 _____

3 _____

4 _____

6 Vocabulary   Hotels and cruise ships

Read the two texts below. One describes a hotel and the other describes a ship. Put the words in the box into the correct spaces in the texts. The first one has been done for you.

cabin service	*chain*	check in	check out	crew
deck	disembark	double rooms	embark	fleet
floor	guests	passengers	porthole	staff
two-berth cabins	window	room service		

a The *Phonecia* is the latest addition to our world-famous ¹ *chain* of luxury hotels. It has over 100 fully equipped ² _____ , and each has a large ³ _____ with a wonderful view of the sea. The facilities include a gymnasium, a cinema, a ballroom, and on the top ⁴ _____ there is a sun garden and swimming pool. There are three restaurants, and we also offer twenty-four-hour ⁵ _____ . From the moment you ⁶ _____ , the ⁷ _____ will be on hand to look after your every need. We pride ourselves on putting our ⁸ _____ first, and are sure that when you ⁹ _____ , you will want to return.

b The *Phonecia* is the latest addition to our world-famous ¹⁰ _____ of luxury liners. It has over 100 fully equipped ¹¹ _____ , and each has a large ¹² _____ with a wonderful view of the sea. The facilities include a gymnasium, a cinema, a ballroom, and on the top ¹³ _____ there is a sun garden and swimming pool. There are three restaurants, and we also offer twenty-four-hour ¹⁴ _____ . From the moment you ¹⁵ _____ , the ¹⁶ _____ will be on hand to look after your every need. We pride ourselves on putting our ¹⁷ _____ first, and are sure that when you ¹⁸ _____ , you will want to return.

7 Writing   A cruise ship

Look at the design of this new cruise ship. You have been asked to write some publicity material describing what the ship will be like and the facilities it will offer. Use your own ideas.

The Emerald Star, which is currently being built in Korea, will be the most luxurious cruise liner ever built. It will have ...

7 Travel by road and rail

1 Talking about preferences

Look at these sentences.

I prefer train travel to coach travel because it's much more comfortable.
I'd rather take the 8.15 than the 9.07 because I want to get to work earlier.
I prefer spending the night in guest-houses to staying in hotels.
I'd rather move on now than stay here for another night.

In which sentences is the speaker talking about:
a a specific choice?
b a general preference?

Write sentences or short paragraphs answering the following questions using your own ideas. Begin with *I'd rather* or *I prefer* and give reasons for your answers. The first one has been done for you.

1 Would you like to work for yourself or for a big travel agency? Why?

   I'd rather work for a big travel agency than for myself because I'd be able to learn more
   about the business, and then maybe I might like to start my own company.

2 On the whole, what do you like more – trains or coaches? Why?

   _____

3 On your next holiday, would you like to stay in a city or in the country? Why?

   _____

4 In general, do you like to travel by car or using public transport?

   _____

5 If you went to the US would you rather have a rail pass or a Greyhound bus pass?

   _____

2 Vocabulary   Road and rail travel

Look at this word train. The words are connected like the carriages of a train – the last letter of one word is the first letter of the next. Most of the words are related to road and rail travel, although there are also some general tourism words and some adjectives for describing characteristics. Clues are listed opposite. The first one has been done for you.

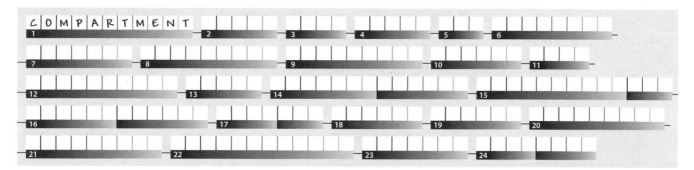

COMPARTMENT

Clues

1 section of a train carriage (11)
2 metal line of rails (5)
3 small metal objects for starting or locking a car (4)
4 the oldest trains used this form of power (5)
5 diagram showing the position of towns, roads, villages, etc. (3)
6 pavement in a station next to the track (8)
7 distance travelled in miles (7)
8 full of energy (9)
9 sleeping berth on a train (9)
10 machine that drives the train (6)
11 way out (4)
12 device in lorry showing details of distance travelled and time of journey (10)
13 building where travellers can rent a room for the night (5)

14 secure container in which you can leave your suitcase or bag (two words: 7,6)
15 part of a train where meals are served (two words: 10,3)
16 ticket from one place to another and back (two words: 6,6)
17 car with driver that you can hire (two words: 4,3)
18 snack bar in a railway station or on a train (6)
19 underground passage through which a train or car can travel (6)
20 large luxurious car (9)
21 moving stairs (9)
22 snacks and drinks (12)
23 train which has beds (7)
24 special card which allows someone to travel free or cheaply (two words: 4,4)

3   **Comparing and contrasting**

A Join up the statements in **a** with the statements in **b** to make a complete sentence. The first one has been done for you.

a *Even though the coach to Madrid was very cheap,*
Not only do you get cheaper travel with a rail pass,
If you travel in low season, it's usually much cheaper;
Even though there wasn't much snow,
She had a great time travelling round Europe,
Suzi Cars only hire out small cars,
Although the flight time from London to Paris is short,
On the one hand, the ferries are very regular,

b on the other hand, they are very slow.
whereas Hertz have a full range of vehicles.
we had a really good skiing holiday.
I don't think we'd do that journey again.
what's more, you avoid the crowds.
but you also get discounts in hotels.
in spite of the weather.
it can take ages to get to and from the airport.

B Rewrite the following sentences using the word or phrase in italics in your answer. This word or phrase does not have to come at the beginning of the sentence. The first one has been done for you.

1 We managed to arrive on time even though the traffic was heavy. *in spite of*

   We managed to arrive on time in spite of the heavy traffic.

2 The coach driver was both incompetent and rude. *but*

   _____

3 Unlike local trains, Intercity Express trains are very fast. *whereas*

   _____

4 We arrived in quite good shape in spite of the length of the journey. *although*

   _____

5 Although the discount is very good, my air pass was very expensive. *in spite of*

   _____

6 The coach is fully air-conditioned and it has an excellent video system. *not only*

   _____

4   Adjectives

A Look at the words in the box. They are all verbs and nouns. Change them into adjectives and put them into the columns below. The first one has been done for you.

beauty	wonder	comfort	dirt	energy
fame	friend	help	hospitality	luxury
noise	panorama	romance	delicacy	tradition
type	enjoy	nation		

Words ending in *-y*   Words ending in *-ic*   Words ending in *-ful*

_____ _____ *beautiful*

_____ _____ _____

_____ _____ _____

Words ending in *-able*   Words ending in *-ous*   Words ending in *-al*

_____ _____ _____

_____ _____ _____

_____ _____ _____

B Read the extract from a publicity leaflet. Then rewrite it, using at least eight of the adjectives above. See the example.

Our coach will take you to see the ruins of Sam Yot.
*Our **comfortable** coach will take you to see the **fabulous** ruins of Sam Yot ...*

_____
_____
_____
_____
_____
_____
_____
_____
_____
_____

The Northern Express will take you from Kuala Lumpur's railway station all the way to the city of Bangkok. If you travel first class you will have the pleasure of staying in a compartment with furniture, and our staff will be on hand to help you with anything you need.
The Northern Express also has a restaurant that serves food, and as you look out, you will be able to enjoy views of the countryside of Malaysia and Thailand.

5

Giving advice

You are working in a travel agency. What advice would you give to your customers in these situations? Use the notes to help you. The first one has been done for you.

1 Mr Young has asked whether a particular villa would be suitable for his family of five for a two-week holiday. (Yes/quite good/noisy road – lots of rooms/a big garden)

   Yes, I think it would be quite good for you. Although it's on quite a noisy road, it has lots of
   rooms and a big garden.

2 Mr and Mrs Graham, aged sixty-five and sixty-seven, want a cheap way to get to Spain from London, and are thinking about going on the overnight coach.

   (No/not a good idea/cheap – very tiring/better alternatives)

   _____

   _____

3 Anna Ward is asking for advice about getting an Inter-rail pass so she can go from London and travel round Europe.

   (Excellent idea/quite expensive – save a lot/go anywhere)

   _____

   _____

4 Mr and Mrs Mason want to travel to Venice in August; they want good weather but dislike crowds.

   (No/not a good idea – weather/fine – very crowded/difficult/find/ accommodation)

   _____

   _____

6

Dealing with problems

Read through the travellers' problems. Using your own ideas, write suitable responses, calming the person down and suggesting a suitable course of action. The first one has been done for you.

1 I can't believe it – I must have picked up someone else's suitcase by mistake.

   There's nothing to worry about. I'll phone the airport and see if your bags are there.

2 I am so scared – there's a horrible hairy spider in the bathroom – I've never seen anything like it.

   _____

3 I can't cope with this car – it's terrible. I've only driven automatics before. It's so difficult.

   _____

4 How can I get home without my passport? I don't know where it is. What am I going to do?

   _____

5 My husband has cut his hand – it's bleeding terribly. There's blood everywhere.

   _____

6 I'm going to miss my connecting flight. I just know it. Oh, no, this is a disaster.

   _____

Negative prefixes

A Match each negative prefix in the middle with the correct group of adjectives on the outside. Then add a negative adjective of your own to each group.

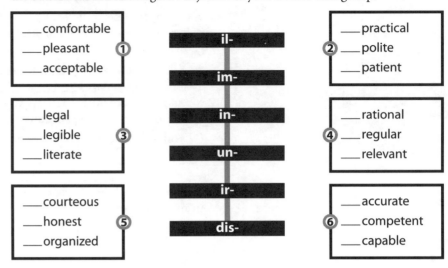

___comfortable ___pleasant ① ___acceptable	___practical ② ___polite ___patient
___legal ___legible ③ ___literate	___rational ④ ___regular ___relevant
___courteous ___honest ⑤ ___organized	___accurate ⑥ ___competent ___capable

il-
im-
in-
un-
ir-
dis-

B Read the following sentences. Fill in the blanks with one of the negative adjectives from **A**. Sometimes more than one answer may be possible. The first one has been done for you.

1 Passengers are reminded that it is _illegal_ to bring pets or other animals into the UK, and that the punishment for anyone doing so is severe.

2 The whole tour was completely _____. The rep was not there to meet us, the hotel was overbooked, and nobody knew what was happening.

3 Could you change the bed in my room? It was so _____ that I didn't get any sleep last night.

4 The description of the facilities in your motorhomes is totally _____, and I suggest you get the errors corrected as soon as possible.

5 I'm not complaining about the colour of the car – that is _____. What I am complaining about is the fact that it is not safe to drive.

6 You cannot seriously expect my wife and I and our four children to sleep in a single room. That is a completely _____ suggestion.

Travel by road and rail

You are a tour representative working for a company taking a group of tourists on a difficult coach tour of ancient Greek monuments. You have just received the following fax from head office.

CLASSICAL TOURS
LONDON
Fax Message

To	Hotel Lakedaiminiko, Sparta, Greece
Attention	---
From	William Warner
Date	18 July
Pages	1
Re	**Tour BC350:** *Golden Age Tour*

I am sorry to hear of the problems you have had with the two passengers, but you seem to have dealt with them well so far.

However, please contact us immediately if there are any further developments, and remember that you have the authority to take any action that you feel is necessary.

Regards

William

Write a fax to William Warner at Head Office. Use the notes below.

1 Lay out the fax correctly.
2 Begin by thanking him for the fax, adding that there have been some more difficulties with the two passengers.
3 Give details of what has happened: explain that you have received complaints from both the hotel staff and the rest of the passengers on the tour.
4 Give details of what action you have taken.
5 End the fax in an appropriate way.

Tickets, reservations, and insurance

1 Vocabulary

Numbers

Write down how you would say the underlined numbers in each of the following pairs of sentences. The first one has been done for you.

1 a There's an afternoon flight that gets in at <u>18.25</u>.

   b The surcharges mean the cost will go up by <u>18.25%</u>.

     eighteen twenty-five

     eighteen point two five per cent

2 a My office number is <u>671 6745</u>.

   b The population of the city is <u>6,716,745</u>.

     _____

     _____

3 a 12.8742 divided by 2.58 = <u>4.99.</u>

   b The cost per person is only <u>£4.99</u>.

     _____

     _____

4 a We opened an office in New York in <u>1997</u>.

   b The exact distance between the cities is <u>1,997</u> km.

     _____

     _____

5 a The average temperature in Greece this month is <u>28°C</u>.

   b In the last five years, our turnover has increased by <u>28%</u>.

     _____

     _____

6 a I usually start work at <u>7.45</u>.

   b 1.12 plus 6.33 equals <u>7.45</u>.

     _____

     _____

7 a A square inch is <u>6.452</u> square centimetres.

   b We have exactly <u>6,452</u> customers on our mailing list.

     _____

     _____

Read through the extract from a brochure. Ten of the adjectives are missing. Reorder the letters in brackets to find the adjectives and write them in the spaces provided. The first one has been done for you.

Source– Thomson Faraway Shores July 97 – October 98 Second Edition Page 201

Mutiara Beach Resort ❶❶❶❶❶   *Penang* Malaysia ▮

Nestled in 18 acres of (torplaci) ¹ *tropical* gardens, this (lurxisouu) ² l_____ hotel fringes one of Penang's (fntise) ³ f_____ sun-kissed beaches. Throughout, the hotel is lavishly furnished with fine attention to detail and all the bedrooms at this hotel enjoy the luxury of either a (gredna) ⁴ g_____ view or sea view. An (ensseld) ⁵ e_____ collection of activities and facilities are available to you however you choose to spend your holiday; whether enjoying a host of sporting pursuits or wining and dining in elegance at one of the hotel's three (secpiytail) ⁶ s_____ restaurants. The (iydcill) ⁷ i_____ beachfront location, the (vadier) ⁸ v_____ facilities, the (fein)

⁹ f_____ service and welcoming atmosphere make the Penang Mutiara Beach resort an (iaedl) ¹⁰ i_____ choice.

Location Beachfront location

Transfer time about 45 minutes

Key features •freshwater swimming pool •children's pool •swim-up bar •2 bars •lounge •3 speciality restaurants (all with no smoking sections) •24 hour coffee shop •weekly barbecue evening •shopping arcade •children's play area

* Special offer:
 10% discount 01 Nov – 11 Dec

Accommodation	Penang Mutiara	
Board Arrangements	Room Only	
Accom. Code	PMU	
Prices based on	Twin for 2	
Nights in Resort	12	19
Adult/Child	Adult	Adult
01 Nov–16 Nov*	959	1195
17 Nov–04 Dec*	939	1175
05 Dec–11 Dec*	929	1165
12 Dec–17 Dec	1189	1425
18 Dec–24 Dec	1279	1515
25 Dec–31 Dec	1209	1445
01 Jan–31 Jan	1069	1305
01 Feb–28 Mar	999	1235
29 Mar–12 Apr	1169	1405
13 Apr–24 Apr	949	1185
01 May–30 May	999	1195
31 May–17 Jun	1039	1235
18 Jun–01 Jul	1099	1295
02 Jul–15 Jul	1159	1355
16 Jul–17 Aug	1199	1395
18 Aug–24 Aug	1119	1315
25 Aug–14 Sep	1079	1275
15 Sep–24 Oct	1059	1255
Supplements per person per night	Single £32.00 B&B £9.80 Half Board £24.80	

Using the information about the Mutiara Beach Resort in Malaysia, write down what you would say to the following customers. Explain how much each part of the holiday would cost and what the total would be.

1 How much would it cost altogether for me to go with my wife for twelve days, half board, leaving at the end of March or the beginning of April?

Well, let's have a look. The basic price …

_____

_____

2 How much would it cost, with bed and breakfast, going and coming back in May and staying for about three weeks? I'm travelling alone, so I would need a single room.

Well, let's have a look. The basic price …

_____

_____

Dates and figures

In the dialogue below a customer at a travel agency is enquiring about a holiday in Malaysia. Using the information about dates and prices from above, put the words from the box below into the correct places in the dialogue. The first one has been done for you.

5th	December	£846	£2,973.20	plus
12th	£24.80	£939	come	special offer
17th	£49.60	£1,189	discount	times
18th	£93	£1,692	include	total
November	£595.20	£2,378	minus	twelve

CUSTOMER   Could you tell me how much it would be for my wife and I to stay at the Mutiara for, say, two weeks?

AGENT   When are you thinking of going?

CUSTOMER   We'd quite like to go in the middle of December.

AGENT   Right, well there are departures on the 12th and the 1 _18th_ of December.

CUSTOMER   How much will it be if we go on the 12th?

AGENT   The basic price is 2 _____ per person.

CUSTOMER   I see, and does that 3 _____ food?

AGENT   No, what would you like – bed and breakfast or half board?

CUSTOMER   Half board, I think.

AGENT   OK, that costs 4 _____ per person per night.

CUSTOMER   Is there anything else – what about things like airport tax and transfers?

AGENT   No, that is all included in the price.

CUSTOMER   OK, so what does that all 5 _____ to?

AGENT   Let's see – two adults leaving on the 12th at £1189 each comes to 6 _____. Then there's half board at £24.80 per person 7 _____ two, which is 8 _____ per night, and that times 9 _____ comes to 10 _____. So the basic price 11 _____ the cost of half board comes to a total of 12 _____.

CUSTOMER   That's expensive. What about if we go before Christmas?

AGENT   Right, let me have a look. Could you go in November?

CUSTOMER   Yes, that would be fine.

AGENT   OK, if you go on the 13 _____ of November, you will get the best deal, because the basic price is only 14 _____ per person. Now, although that's ten more than the departure on the 15 _____ of December, there's a 16 _____ for anyone departing and returning between the 1st of 17 _____ and the 11th of 18 _____, and that means that you'll get a 19 _____ of 20 _____ per person.

CUSTOMER   So what would all that come to – and let's say we don't have bed and breakfast or half board. We can probably eat out quite cheaply.

AGENT   Yes, I'm sure you can. Let's just work that out – £939 21 _____ £93 comes to 22 _____ per person, so that times two makes a 23 _____ of 24 _____.

CUSTOMER   That's much better.

You are a travel agent and your two customers, Mr Petersen and Mr Nils, are Dutch executives currently in London. They are planning to go to Nairobi on 21 September, and can leave any time after 8 a.m. Mr Nils has asked you to contact KLM's flight information web site on the Internet for the latest information.

A Complete the boxes below with the information requested about your customers and their travel requirements.

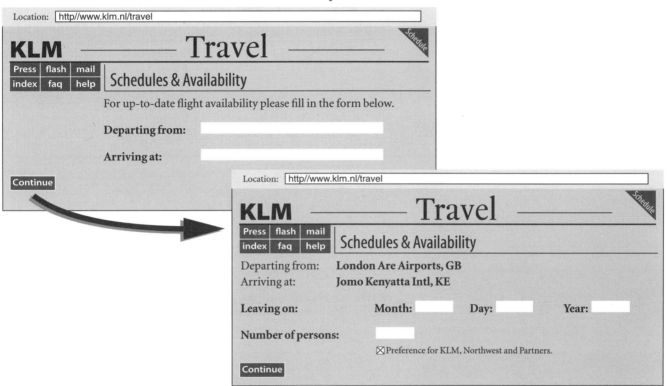

Location: http//www.klm.nl/travel

KLM ——— Travel ———

Press | flash | mail
index | faq | help

Schedules & Availability

For up-to-date flight availability please fill in the form below.

Departing from:

Arriving at:

Continue

Location: http//www.klm.nl/travel

KLM ——— Travel ———

Press | flash | mail
index | faq | help

Schedules & Availability

Departing from: **London Are Airports, GB**
Arriving at: **Jomo Kenyatta Intl, KE**

Leaving on: **Month:** ___   **Day:** ___   **Year:** ___

Number of persons: ___

☒ Preference for KLM, Northwest and Partners.

Continue

B Read the information you receive back.

Location: http//www.klm.nl/travel

KLM ——— Travel ———

Airline Flight	Departure Arrival	Origin Destination	Airplane	Availability First	Bus.	Econ.
		*Operated by a codeshare partner airline.				
Kenya Airways KQ101	20:10 Sep 22, 1997 / 06:55 Sep 23, 1997	Heathrow / Jomo Kenyatta Intl	Airbus A310	n.a.	yes	n.a.
KLM KL114	08:35 Sep 21, 1997 / 10:45 Sep 21, 1997	Heathrow / Schiphol Arpt	Boeing 767	n.a.	yes	yes
KLM KL535	12:40 Sep 21, 1997 / 19:45 Sep 21, 1997	Schiphol Arpt / Jeddah Intl	Boeing 767	n.a.	yes	yes
Saudi Arabian SV447	02:50 Sep 22, 1997 / 06:25 Sep 22, 1997	Jeddah Intl / Jomo Kenyatta Intl	Airbus AB3	yes	n.a.	yes
KLM KL122	14:20 Sep 21, 1997 / 16:30 Sep 21, 1997	Heathrow / Schiphol Arpt	Boeing 767	n.a.	yes	yes
Egyptair MS882	17:45 Sep 21, 1997 / 23:45 Sep 21, 1997	Schiphol Arpt / Cairo Intl Arpt	Boeing 767	n.a.	yes	n.a.
Egyptair MS759	01:45 Sep 22, 1997 / 06:30 Sep 22, 1997	Cairo Intl Arpt / Jomo Kenyatta Intl	Airbus AB3	n.a.	yes	yes

View flights   previous day   next day   **Return to** selection.

We do everything possible to ensure that this timetable presents the latest schedule and availability information. However, we recommend that you have all flight details confirmed before making reservations for your personal itinerary. Availability of seats may not be applicable for all fare types.

C Now use this information to answer your client's questions. Complete the dialogue below.

NILS	Are there any direct flights to Nairobi on the 21st?
TRAVEL AGENT	No, there aren't. The only direct flight leaves on the 22nd and gets in at 06.55 on the 23rd.
NILS	I see. Who's that with?
TRAVEL AGENT	1 _____
NILS	That would be OK. Presumably they have seats in Business Class?
TRAVEL AGENT	2 _____
NILS	I'd rather go Business Class on a long flight like that, and anyway we'd arrive a day late. What is the next option?
TRAVEL AGENT	3 _____
NILS	So that would involve two changes. How much time would we have at Schipol?
TRAVEL AGENT	4 _____
NILS	And what about in Jeddah?
TRAVEL AGENT	5 _____
NILS	That's quite a long time to be sitting in the airport. Anyway, are there seats available in Business Class on all the flights?
TRAVEL AGENT	6 _____
NILS	I'm not sure it would be worth the extra cost. Are there any other options?
TRAVEL AGENT	7 _____
NILS	So that would still involve two changes. What are the transfer times like?
TRAVEL AGENT	8 _____
NILS	That's a bit better. Sorry, when did you say it left Heathrow?
TRAVEL AGENT	9 _____
NILS	At least that would give us the morning in London. Are there seats in Business Class all the way?
TRAVEL AGENT	10 _____
NILS	And what about the arrival time compared to the flight via Jeddah?
TRAVEL AGENT	11 _____
NILS	OK, that sounds the best option. I'll get in touch with my colleague and call you back.

Describing events in the past

A Read this extract from an insurance claim. Put the verbs in brackets into the simple past, past perfect, or past continuous. The first one has been done for you.

I am fairly sure that the theft [1] _took_ (take) place while [2] _____ (have) breakfast. In fact, on my way back to the room, I [3] _____ (pass) a man who was about twenty-five years old who [4] _____ (behave) rather strangely, and who [5] _____ (hold) some sort of bag in his hand. Anyway, as soon as I [6] _____ (get) to my room, I [7] _____ (knew) at once that someone [8] _____ (be) in there – the drawer [9] _____ (lie) on the floor and my traveller's cheques and passport [10] _____ (steal). Then, while I [11] _____ (look) around, I [12] _____ (realize) that the souvenirs and presents I [13] _____ (buy) the day before were missing as well.

B Complete each of the following sentences in three different ways, using your own ideas. Write sentences using the simple past, past continuous, and past perfect. The first one has been done for you

1 When the coach broke down   ... *we had just passed a small village.*
                                    ... *we were driving from Grenada to Malaga.*
                                    ... *the driver phoned the company.*

2 When I finally got to the airport   ...
                                       ...
                                       ...

3 When the fire broke out   ...
                                       ...
                                       ...

4 When the police arrived at the hotel ...
                                       ...
                                       ...

7 Writing   An accident

Look at the following pictures. Write a report for an insurance company explaining how the accident happened and what you lost, giving as much detail as possible.

9

Tourist information

1 Vocabulary   Tourist attractions and facilities

A In the box below are the names of different types of tourist attractions. The letters have been mixed up. Reorder them and put each one into the correct space in the postcard. The first one has been done for you.

Dear Charlene

Having a great time and seeing all the sights. On the first day we visited the famous ¹ _cathedral_ of Saint Basil and then spent the afternoon looking at the paintings in the Tretyakov ² _____. The kids got a bit bored with all the culture, but they enjoyed looking at the weapons and armoury in the Kremlin ³ _____ the following day. We also found a great ⁴ _____ park for the younger ones with cartoon characters and rides and everything right near the city centre. Today we checked out the ⁵ _____ on Arbat Street and bought lots of great souvenirs. I can't believe that tomorrow is our last night already. We're hoping to take in an opera or a ballet at the Bolshoi ⁶ _____ and maybe go for a meal in a traditional ⁷ _____. The older kids are going out to a ⁸ _____ with some friends they made.

Anyway, see you soon.

Bobby

ehaettr	tgihn lucb
rta lrgylea	nuttsaarree
strosref	*rdcahldet*
emthe	alef ekrmat

Charlene Smith

126 London Road

Bath

ENGLAND

B Read the postcard again. Can you work out which city the writer is in? _____

2   Additional information clauses

Read the following passage about a market in New Orleans. Fill in the blanks with the words in the box. You will need to use some of the words more than once. The first one has been done for you.

who   which   when   where   whose

• The French Market, [1] *which* is situated in Esplanade Street, is America's oldest market and was originally used by the Choctaw Indians, [2] _____ lived in the area long before the Europeans settled.

• The original buildings, [3] _____ were put up by the Spanish in 1771, stood until 1812, [4] _____ they were destroyed by a hurricane. Soon afterwards the market was rebuilt and the buildings that stand today date from the early 19th century.

• The fruit and meat vendors, [5] _____ stalls are in the main building, always start work early. You should try and visit in the morning, [6] _____ you will find restaurateurs, grocers and others haggling over the best produce. At the weekends the French Market is transformed into a giant flea market, [7] _____ you can buy just about anything you want.

3   Tourist attractions in New Orleans

Read these sentences about other places of interest in New Orleans. Join the sentences together using extra information clauses beginning with *who*, *which*, *where*, *whose*, or *when*. Remember to use commas at the beginning of each relative clause. The first one has been done for you.

CONFEDERATE MUSEUM

a The Confederate Museum is the oldest museum in Louisiana.
It was built in 1891.

The museum has a large art gallery.
You can see pictures of the Civil War there.

Included in the collection are the personal effects of General Robert E. Lee.
General Lee was the leader of the Confederate army.

DESTREHANE PLANTATION

b The Destrehane Plantation is conveniently located near the city.
It is the oldest in Louisiana.

It was originally built by the d'Estrehan family.
The family were French aristocrats.

It's a great place to visit in November.
The annual festival is held in November.

LONGUE VUE HOUSE

c Longue Vue House is a beautiful English-style country home.
It is set in eight acres of beautiful countryside.

It originally belonged to the Stern family.
The Stern family's collection of modern art is still housed there.

The estate has beautiful gardens.
You can have picnics and relax there.

1 *The Confederate Museum, which was built in 1891, is the oldest museum in Louisiana.*

2 _____

3 _____

4 _____

5 _____

6 _____

7 _____

8 _____

9 _____

Tourist attractions in Canberra

Read the text about tourist attractions and facilities in Canberra, Australia. Some lines are correct, and some contain an extra word. If the line is correct, put a tick (✔) next to it. If the line is wrong, underline the word you do not need. The first two have been done for you.

Theatre

The Canberra Theatre Centre, in the heart of the city,   ✔

provides performances <u>all</u> throughout the year. There are many other   *all*

theatre venues and, depending on the season, outdoor side performances   _____

and street theatre as well . For details of what's being on during your stay, _____

check the entertainment section of Thursday's *Canberra Times*.   _____

Cinema

There are also have seven cinema complexes. At the Electric Shadows   _____

cinema in the city, you can catch up on classics and on the latest releases.   _____

If you're a film buff, you mustn't to miss the chance of browsing in their   _____

bookshop – it's one of the most best in the country.   _____

Clubs

For an inexpensive night out, visit to one of our licensed clubs.   _____

The facilities include restaurants and bars offering an excellent value for   _____

money. Casino Canberra is a European-style 'boutique' casino – which it   _____

means it's small enough to give you excellent service, and big enough for   _____

to offer world-class facilities. Whether you're a first-timer or a high-roller, _____

the friendly staff will make sure you feel at the home.   _____

5 Writing

Tourist attractions in your area

You have been asked to write a leaflet describing some tourist attractions or facilities in an area you know well. You should provide information that will interest the following groups of people:

1 families with young children
2 people interested in culture
3 foreign students looking for a fun night out.

Complete the paragraphs below. The first one (for families with young children) has been done for you.

1 Family entertainment

If you're looking for somewhere to take the kids, why not pay a visit to the Cotswold Wildlife Park. There is a wonderful collection of animals, ranging from rhinos and tigers to parrots and penguins. There's an enchanting walled garden, an adventure playground, and a small farmyard where children are encouraged to touch the animals. The park is open every day except 25 December.

2 Museums and galleries

If museums and art galleries are what interest you most, then you can't leave without visiting …

_____

_____

_____

3 Night-life

If you're looking for a fun night out with friends, why not …

_____

_____

_____

6   Hotel facilities

Emerald Beach Motel
14701 Front Beach Road
Panama City Beach, FL 32413

Now you can find something of great value right here on Panama City Beach

		1 bed	2 beds	2 beds+ kitchen	2 rooms 3 beds + kitchen
	Adults	2	2	2	4
Mar 1– Apr 12	day	$55	$79	$89	$99
	week	$355	$450	$535	$595
Apr13 – May 15	day	$45	$59	$69	$79
	week	$270	$360	$420	$480
May 16– June 5	day	$55	$69	$79	$89
	week	$355	$450	$525	$595
June 6– Sept 2	day	$65	$85	$95	$105
	week	$425	$550	$615	$675
Back to School Special					
Aug 17– Aug 28	day	$40	$60	$70	$80
	week	$240	$360	$420	$480

Additional adults $7.00 per night or $42 per week.
Crib or rollaway bed $5.00 per night
or $30 per week. Infants (under 2) free.
Children (2–16) 50% of adult rate

You are working in a tourist information office in Panama and a tourist has phoned for information about hotels. Read the information and complete the dialogue.

YOU   I think that the Emerald Beach Motel would probably suit you best.

TOURIST   OK, can you tell me a little more about it? How far is it from the sea?

YOU   1 _____

TOURIST   Oh, good. Now, how much does it cost?

YOU   2 _____

TOURIST   Well, there's myself, my wife and our two children.

YOU   3 _____

TOURIST   One is four and the other is fifteen months.

YOU   4 _____

TOURIST   Yes, we'd want to share a room, but we'd need a crib and an extra bed.

YOU   5 _____

TOURIST   Yes, a room with a kitchen would be perfect.

YOU   6 _____

TOURIST   We're planning to come on the 20th of May, and we'd like to stay for eight days. Do you know how much that would all come to?

YOU   7 _____

TOURIST   That sounds quite reasonable. I'll have a word with my wife and get back to you, OK?

7   Simple past active or passive

Read the following passage about the Panama Canal. Put the verbs into the simple past active or passive. The first one has been done for you.

The Panama Canal is one of the most significant engineering achievements of the twentieth century, but it was a project that took over 500 years to finally complete.

The first proposal to build a canal ¹ _was put_____ (put) forward in 1523. Charles V of Spain ² _____ (order) a survey of the area, but no action ³ _____ (take). More than three centuries ⁴ _____ (pass) before a new attempt ⁵ _____ (make). A French company, under the leadership of Ferdinand de Lesseps,

who ⁶ _____ (build) the Suez Canal, ⁷ _____ (work) on the project for twenty years. They ⁸ _____ (begin) in 1880, but ⁹ _____ (defeat) by disease and financial problems.

In 1906, President Roosevelt ¹⁰ _____ (order) the US Army Corps of Engineers to begin construction, and the project ¹¹ _____ (control) by Colonel Goethals. During the project, about 143 million cubic metres of earth ¹² _____ (remove), and the entire area, which ¹³ _____ (infest) with malaria-carrying mosquitoes, had to be sanitized. It ¹⁴ _____ (estimate) that the project would take ten years, but in fact the work ¹⁵ _____ (complete) in the summer of 1914 at a cost of about $336 million.

The canal, which links the Pacific and Atlantic ocean, is just over sixty-four kilometres long. The minimum depth is 12.5m, and the minimum width is 91.5m.

8   **Dimensions**

A The letters of the words below have been mixed up. Reorder them to make the names of four famous places or structures.

> gtaer rampdiy   chlenna utelnn   gdenlo agte bgedir   apaman anlac

B The texts below describe the four famous places or structures from **A**. Write in the name of the place or structure described. Then put the words in the box into the correct place in the texts. You will need to use some of the words more than once.

> long   length   wide   width   high   height   deep   depth

1 _____

Overall, it is 50.4 km long, and consists of three separate tunnels. The two main ones are 7.6m _____, and the _____ of the central service tunnel is 4.8m. The overall _____ of the undersea section is 39 km.

2 _____

It is suspended from two towers, each of which are 227.4 m _____, and the overall _____ of the central span is 1280.2m.

3 _____

The original _____ of the structure was 147m, but it is now slightly lower as some of the top stones have been removed. At the base, each of the four sides is 230m _____ .

4 _____

It is a little more than 64km _____, and with a minimum _____ of 12.5 m, it is _____ enough to allow large vessels. It has a minimum _____ of 91.5m, allowing vessels to pass each other at any stage.

9 Reading   A job at a leisure attraction

A The following article is about working at a leisure attraction. Some of the sentences have been removed. Read through the text and put the sentences below into the correct places. There is one extra sentence which you will not need. The first one has been done for you.

a You may be expected to work shifts and weekends but you will find great satisfaction watching and helping others enjoy themselves.

b They also get the chance to try the rides for free.

c *Today, you can also be employed as a 'pirate' or a 'wild west cowboy', and these jobs are exciting, challenging, and ... different!*

d However, once you begin to specialize in a water world or a museum, you will have to be trained.

e It's important that you are able to keep going, regardless of how you feel.

f Later in your career you could become a manager of one or more sections or departments.

g Why not find out more about the opportunities open to you?

►►OPPORTUNITIES
► *in leisure attractions*

All about the job

People visit leisure attractions for a variety of reasons; it could be for the view, for the ride, for learning, or just for the experience. Whichever attraction they choose, people take their leisure time seriously, and their expectations for quality and service are always high. So, whether you work in an historic building, a theme park, a museum, or a water world, you will be helping to satisfy people's dreams and expectations.

All leisure attractions need catering staff, but if you're technically minded, there are also jobs for electricians, plumbers, carpenters, and ground staff. **1** _c_. What brings them together is the need for you to be able to help others enjoy themselves, either for an hour, for a day, or sometimes even longer.

Whether you want to work for the whole year, a season, weekends, or evenings, the choice is yours. **2**___. You must always deliver to your guests the 'experience' that they have chosen and paid for.

The great outdoors

Many leisure attractions are, of course, based around outdoor activities, but there are just as many inside, and the weather and the time of year will have an effect upon both the numbers of visitors and on you. You need a good personality to cope outdoors in the rain, as you do indoors in the heat of the summer. Hours vary and can often be long. **3**___.

Qualifications and training

Usually, no specific qualifications are needed to get started in the leisure industry. **4**___. Sometimes your company will also expect you to take examinations, for example life-saving, and continual 'on-the-job' training is always given to keep you informed.

For support services, and those jobs requiring professional knowledge, you may need to obtain external examinations, but again many companies will help.

Where to after training?

Starting as a trainee or a summer casual you could develop and become, with training and experience, a team leader or a supervisor. **5**___.

Are you right for the job?

If you want to help people enjoy themselves and have a lively personality, then a job in a leisure attraction could be for you. **6**___.

OPPORTUNITIES

B Advantages and disadvantages

Which of the following points are mentioned in the text? Write *Yes* or *No*. The first one has been done for you.

1 There are a wide variety of jobs available in leisure attractions. _Yes_
2 Visitors are often aggressive and demanding. ___
3 You can choose when you want to work. ___
4 You have be enthusiastic even if you are not feeling well. ___
5 The weather can sometimes make the work difficult. ___
6 You may have to work long or inconvenient hours. ___
7 You don't need any special qualifications to get your first job. ___
8 You will have to pass some difficult examinations. ___
9 The salaries are very low. ___
10 Some jobs offer a good career structure. ___

C Write two short paragraphs, based on the information above, explaining the advantages and disadvantages of working in the leisure industry.

10

Guiding

1

Personal qualities

A Look through this list of personal qualities. Arrange them into three lists. Say which, in your opinion, are **a** – always good, **b** – sometimes good, **c** – always bad. The first three have been done for you.

approachable	*aggressive*	*ambitious*	well-informed
arrogant	attractive	assertive	confident
domineering	shy	enthusiastic	friendly
highly intelligent	untrustworthy	patronizing	rude

a	**b**	**c**
approachable	*ambitious*	*aggressive*
_____	_____	_____
_____	_____	_____
_____	_____	_____
_____	_____	_____
_____	_____	_____

B Now choose six of the words above, and complete the following sentences about the qualities you need to be a good guide, giving your reasons. See the example.

A good guide has to be well-informed about the place she is visiting so that she can interest the group and answer any questions they may have.

1 A good guide needs to be _____
_____.

2 A good guide has to be _____
_____.

3 A good guide doesn't have to be _____
_____.

4 A good guide doesn't need to be _____
_____.

5 A guide shouldn't be _____
_____.

6 A guide mustn't be _____
_____.

Telephone language

A tour operator is phoning a guide to see if she can do some work. Read the guide's half of their conversation.

Hello, Mary Danzig.

1 _____

Oh, hello, nice to hear from you again. What can I do for you?

2 _____

I'll just get my diary and you can give me the details. OK, go ahead.

3 _____

Would it be the same as I did last year in the open-top bus?

4 _____

Good, so I might be able to use the commentary I prepared last time – but what sort of group is it?

5 _____

Oh good, so there won't be any language problems. Now, when would you like me to do it?

6 _____

That's fine by me – I'm free then. Have you got anything in mind for later on?

7 _____

OK, let me take a note of that. By the way, what play is it?

8 _____

Right – and do you want me to book a restaurant?

9 _____

Thanks very much. Goodbye.

The sentences below are the tour operator's half of the conversation. Put them into the correct places in the dialogue above.

a Right, the first part is an afternoon tour of historic London.
b Yes, that's right, and the route is still the same.
c Hello, this is Brian from Heritage Tours.
d No, that's OK, we've arranged it all, but it might be a good idea to confirm it. Anyway, I'll send you all the details, and give me a ring if there's anything else you need to know.
e There will be about fifteen people in all – they're mainly the wives of some American businessmen who are here for a week or so.
f Yes, it will be followed by a theatre trip and dinner.
g Well, I was wondering if you would be able to do a tour for us.
h Next Wednesday, that's the eighteenth.
i It's a musical – *Cats*. We've got tickets.

Word formation

A Read the description of a five-day opera tour. The words below have been removed from the text. They are in the right order but not in the right form. Choose the correct form of the word to fill in the gaps in the text. The first one has been done for you.

1 *idyll*	5 relax	9 perform	13 beauty
2 celebrate	6 architect	10 fine	14 option
3 history	7 wonder	11 shop	15 arrive
4 luxury	8 arrange	12 question	

Every summer the ancient Roman arena in the centre of Verona is the ¹ *idyllic* _____ *setting for the* ² _____ *Italian Opera. Our short break includes two evenings of opera, time to enjoy Vicenza and a day to savour the* ³ _____ *city of Venice.*

OPERA & ITALY

Day 1 We depart locally for London Heathrow Airport and your flight to Milan. Our coach will transfer you to the ⁴ _____ Forte Agip Hotel in Vicenza. Evening free to settle in and enjoy a ⁵ _____ dinner.

Day 2 Today you are free to explore Vicenza, home of the Palladian style of ⁶ _____. Later in the day we board our coach for the easy drive to Verona for dinner and a ⁷ _____ evening of opera at the Roman Arena. ⁸ _____ have been made for you to have very good seats (second sector stalls). After the ⁹ _____ our coach takes us back to the Forte Agip Vicenza.

Day 3 Late morning we take the short drive to Verona, after Venice the ¹⁰ _____ art centre in Venetia. It is an elegant city with excellent ¹¹ _____ opportunities. Dinner at the Forte Agip Verona before taking our seats for another delightful evening of opera in the Roman Arena. Overnight at the Forte Agip Vicenza.

Day 4 Today we board our coach for the journey to Venice, ¹² _____ one of the world's most ¹³ _____ cities. Day free to explore at leisure, or you may join us on one of our ¹⁴ _____ guided tours.

Day 5 After breakfast we transfer you to Venice Airport for your scheduled Alitalia flight to London Gatwick Airport. On ¹⁵ _____ our staff will greet you and transfer you for your homeward journey.

B Imagine that you were the guide on the tour to Italy above. Read the text again and answer the following questions from the members of the group. The first one has been done for you.

1 Does Vicenza have an airport?

No, we'll be arriving at Milan, and then we'll take a coach to our hotel in Vicenza.

2 Are we doing anything on the first evening?

_____

3 Is Vicenza famous for anything?

_____

4 Are we seeing any operas in Vicenza?

_____

5 Is it very far to Verona?

_____

6 When will we have a chance to explore Verona?

_____

7 Will we be going round Venice as a group?

_____

8 How are we going to get back to Milan airport?

_____

10

Guiding

Look at the following fax giving details of some of your instructions and the notes you have made. Then complete the task below.

Day 2

Group meets at 12.30 at ~~La Ristorante~~ for lunch.

16.30 Board coach for Verona. Agnelli's Coaches Tel: 0239 43 95 47

18.00 Dinner at Angelino's.

20.00 Performance of Cosi fan tutti. Collect tickets at door.

23.30 Board coach, return to Verona. Pay driver gratuity (£10).

You need the information above, but the people you need to contact are out of the office. Write down what message you would leave on the answering machines. The first one has been done for you as an example.

Message 1 You phone your Head Office as the fax message was unclear. Find out which restaurant you are meant to be going to.

Hello, this is Janie Mitchell in Vicenza doing the opera tour. I'm afraid the name of the restaurant we're meant to be having lunch in tomorrow didn't come through on the fax you sent me. Could you let me know what it is and whether I need to confirm the reservation? You can call me at the hotel and leave a message or send a fax to the hotel on 0239 77 33 44. Thank you.

Message 2 You phone Agnelli's coaches to confirm that the pick-up point will be at the hotel. You also want to know if the same driver is bringing you back.

_____
_____
_____

Message 3 You phone the restaurant to confirm the reservations.

_____
_____
_____

Message 4 You phone the ticket office to check arrangements for picking up the tickets.

_____
_____
_____

5

Adjectives ending in -*ed* and -*ing*

An examiner who assesses guides is talking about some of the qualities that a good guide needs to have. Fill in the blanks with the words in brackets in either the -*ed* form or the -*ing* form.

The most important quality that we are looking for is the ability of the guide to give an [1] _____ (interest) talk – no tour is going to be successful if the audience is [2] _____ (bore), however [3] _____ (fascinate) the place they are visiting may be.

The guides have to have a clear idea of what they are going to say. Preparation is very important because no audience is going to be [4] _____ (satisfy) with a long, [5] _____ (confuse) commentary that has not been thought out properly.

Guides should also know about microphone technique and how to address the audience and it is [6] _____ (surprise) how many candidates who come here for examinations have problems with this. It can be very [7] _____ (annoy) if the guide does not speak into the microphone, and guides need to learn to stand still and avoid too many hand gestures, which can be very [8] _____ (distract).

As people, guides need to appear confident and [9] _____ (relax), and need to know when to lighten the commentary with an [10] _____ (amuse) story or anecdote. Long tours can be [11] _____ (exhaust), and it is important to realize when people are getting [12] _____ (tire), and to change the pace of a commentary as necessary.

6

Strong and weak adjectives

Some adjectives can be made stronger by using words like *very*, *extremely*, etc. Other adjectives already have a strong meaning, and can only be made stronger by using words like *absolutely*.

A Look through this list of adjectives and put them into two columns. The first two have been done for you.

interesting	*fascinating*	wonderful	nice	fantastic	magnificent
impressive	terrible	appalling	good	brilliant	famous
old	elegant	attractive	bad	long	superb

Neutral adjectives

(*very …*
extremely …)

interesting

_____

_____

_____

_____

_____

Strong adjectives

(*absolutely …*)

fascinating

_____

_____

_____

_____

_____

B Read the following sentences. Choose which of the words in italics is correct and underline it.

1 The history of the building is absolutely *interesting/fascinating*.
2 Notice the extremely *elegant/magnificent* pillars at the front of the church.
3 The story of what happened in the tower is absolutely *frightening/terrifying*.
4 The Bible that is on display here is *very/absolutely* old.
5 The architect Inigo Jones had a *very/absolutely* long and distinguished career.
6 The staircase that leads up to the front door is very *impressive/fantastic*.

7 Writing task

The Tower of London

A Below are some notes about the Tower of London. They are mixed up. Arrange the notes into three topic areas.

We are now about to enter the 'Bloody Tower'.
We are now entering the Jewel House.
We are now entering the Chapel of St John.
It is called the Bloody Tower because of the deaths of two young princes.
The chapel is one of the most beautiful buildings in England.
The princes were the sons of Edward IV, who died in 1483.
The royal crowns and other treasures are on display here.
They were kept in here by their uncle Richard, Duke of Gloucester.
Richard later became king.
The chapel dates from 1080.
The greatest treasure is the Imperial State Crown.
The chapel contains a perfect barrel vault.
This is worn by the monarch on major state occasions.
He is thought to have murdered the princes.
The vault is built of Caen stone.
The bodies were never found.
The vault is extremely well preserved.
The crown is encrusted with 2,800 diamonds.
The crown is set with several historic gemstones.

B Now use the notes to write a guide's commentary for the three areas of the Tower of London.

1 _____
_____
_____

2 _____
_____
_____

3 _____
_____
_____

Promotion and marketing in tourism

1 Great marketing disasters

A When you decide to promote a product, it is possible to make mistakes without realizing it. Read the following incomplete texts. Then look at **B**.

When Braniff Airlines changed the seat covers in their aeroplanes and used leather rather than man-made fabrics, they launched a new advertising slogan – 'Fly in leather'.

a

A new airline company decided to call itself 'EMU', and had some success until it tried to market its services in Australia. It took some time before they realized that the name wasn't appropriate.

b

When an American food company launched a new range of baby food in Africa, they put a picture of a smiling baby on each tin so that it could be identified. They were a little surprised when the product did not seem to be selling well.

c

The vacuum cleaner company Hoover had a marketing disaster from a campaign that went too well. They offered customers two free flights to America (worth £400) if they bought any product worth over £100.

d

Brand names can cause problems for international companies. When the car company Chevrolet produced a new model, they decided to call it the 'Nova'.

e

B Below are the continuations of the texts in **A**. Match the two halves of each story.

1 They realized their mistake when it was explained to them that in many areas where people cannot read or write, people assumed that the picture on the label showed what was in the tin.

2 An emu is a native Australian bird, but unfortunately, rather like an ostrich, it can't fly.

3 This slogan was translated into different languages, but raised a few laughs in Spain, where the translation meant 'Fly naked'.

4 People soon realized that this was a very good deal indeed. The company sold vast quantities of appliances and ended up with a loss of £48 million.

5 It was fine in most countries except in Spain, where *no* means *doesn't* and *va* means *go*.

2 First and second conditionals

Read through the following sentences.

a *If there are any seats available, I'll book you a ticket for the 21st.*
b *If there were any seats available, I would book you a ticket for the 21st.*

In which sentence is the speaker talking about a real possibility?
In which sentence is the speaker talking about an imaginary situation?

Remember that we use the first conditional to talk about future events and their results when the future event is reasonably likely to happen. For example:
If I have to stay late this evening, I will give you a ring.

We use the second conditional to talk about the results of imaginary present situations or unlikely future events. For example:
If I had a yacht, I would spend the summer in the West Indies.

A Complete the sentences using either the first conditional or the second conditional.

1 If the economy _____ (not/be) in such a bad state, it _____ (be) much easier to sell holidays.

2 If I _____ (have) more money I _____ (spend) the summer in the South of France, but unfortunately I have to stay here.

3 Nobody _____ (mind) if the plane _____ (be) a few minutes late.

4 I'm expecting the tickets any time now – I _____ (phone) you if they _____ (come) tomorrow.

5 If I _____ (be) you, I _____ (complain) to the tour operator.

6 It's a shame we haven't got anything to spend on promotion. If we _____ (have) a little spare cash, we _____ (be able) to advertise and get a lot of customers.

7 It's a pity I don't speak Turkish. If I _____ (do), I _____ (apply) for that job in Istanbul.

8 If you _____ (have) any problems, our local representative _____ (do) her best to help you and can be contacted at any time.

B Read the following questions, and write a suitable reply. Choose the first conditional to talk about the suggestion you support, and the second conditional to talk about the suggestion you do not support. The first one has been done for you.

1 We're opening a new chain of hotels for business travellers all over Europe. Do you think we should promote them by giving out leaflets in the street or by setting up an Internet web site?

I think a web site would be better – if we set one up we will be able to reach customers all over the world, but if we just handed out leaflets we wouldn't get the right sort of customers.

2 We have a lot of late availability flights to sell – do you think we should put an advertisement in the paper or get some posters put up in the underground?

_____

_____

3 We're trying to get some publicity for our 18–30 adventure holidays. Do you think we should think about sponsoring a sports event or take out advertisements in a theatre programme?

_____

_____

4 We're opening a new branch in West Street – do you think we should organize a TV campaign or get some leaflets printed to hand out in the street?

_____

_____

3

Adjectives

A Match the sets of adjectives with the word in the centre that each one can describe. The first one has been done for you.

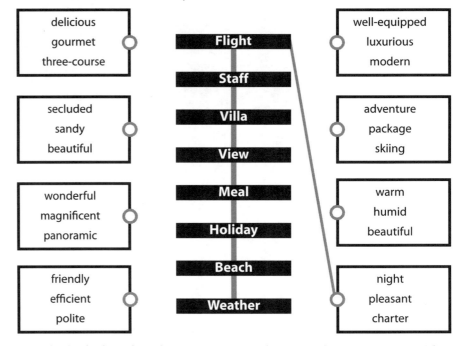

delicious
gourmet
three-course

secluded
sandy
beautiful

wonderful
magnificent
panoramic

friendly
efficient
polite

Flight
Staff
Villa
View
Meal
Holiday
Beach
Weather

well-equipped
luxurious
modern

adventure
package
skiing

warm
humid
beautiful

night
pleasant
charter

B Now think of at least five adjective + noun combinations that you associate with the types of holiday below. The first one has been done for you.

1 **a skiing holiday**

guaranteed snow   traditional chalet   exhilarating runs   lively nightclubs   expert instruction

2 **a safari**

_____

3 **a trekking holiday**

_____

4 **a package holiday**

_____

4

Selling holidays

Imagine you are trying to sell two of the holidays to customers. Write down what you would say about each of the holidays they are interested in, using your ideas from exercise 3. The first one has been done for you.

1 *I'm sure you'd enjoy the skiing holiday in Wengen – you'd stay in a traditional chalet that is very clean and comfortable, and is close to the slopes. The skiing is first class, because there is guaranteed snow. There are some exhilarating runs and you can also get expert instruction. And the après–ski is great, because Wengen has some excellent restaurants and lively nightclubs.*

2 _____

_____

_____

_____

3 _____

_____

_____

_____

Superlatives and ranking

A Use the following constructions to make the groups of words below into sentences. The first one has been done for you.

The cathedral is	the one of the the second the third etc.	oldest most popular	tourist attraction(s) in the state.

1 Christ Church/large/college/Oxford.
   Christ Church is the largest college in Oxford.

2 St Petersburg/beautiful/city/Russia.

   _____

3 Thomas Cook/one of/famous/travel agencies/world.

   _____

4 Chichen Itza/one of/ancient/site/Central America.

   _____

5 Birmingham/no.2/big/city/England.

   _____

6 Kanchenjunga/no.3/high/mountain/world

   _____

7 Dhaulagiri/no.7/high/peak/Nepal

   _____

B Using your own ideas, say what you know about the following places and people.
   1 The Taj Mahal

   _____

   2 The Grand Canyon

   _____

   3 The Eiffel Tower

   _____

   4 The Empire State Building (The phrase *used to be* could be helpful.)

   _____

   5 Bill Gates

   _____

   6 Yourself

   _____

A The following is an extract from a travel brochure about trekking in Nepal. Some of the words have been removed. Read the text and then look at **B**.

NEPAL
lodge treks

ANNAPURNA CIRCUIT
24 DAYS   **GRADE C**

Lodges
ASK FOR DOSSIER TNQ

24 days Tue to Thu			
Ref	Start	End	£
TNQ711	11 Mar '97	03 Apr	1175
TNQ712	18 Mar	10 Apr	1175
TNQ713	25 Mar	17 Apr	1175
TNQ740	30 Sep	23 Oct	1175
TNQ741	07 Oct	30 Oct	1175
TNQ742	14 Oct	06 Nov	1175
TNQ743	21 Oct	13 Nov	1175
TNQ744	28 Oct	20 Nov	1175
TNQ811	10 Mar '98	02 Apr	1175
TNQ813	24 Mar	16 Apr	1175
TNQ814	31 Mar	23 Apr	1175
Insurance £61			

Nepal's classic trek, with an amazing variety of scenery and culture.

This circuit of Annapurna – rightly [1] _known_ as Nepal's classic trek – offers more variety than any other walk of equivalent length, and takes us through virtually every type of scenery that Nepal has to [2] _____. There are superb views of Annapurna and Dhaulagiri. The constant [3] _____ of landscapes ranges from sub-tropical through Alpine to an arid semi-desert akin to Tibet, and at the climax of the trek there's a mighty 5,316m pass, the Thorong La, to cross.

This is a lodge-based trek, so we spend time in villages inhabited by many of Nepal's different tribes, both Bhuddist and Hindu. Though it is certainly demanding [4] _____ for the seasoned trekker, the Annnapurna circuit is still an excellent [5] _____ to walking in Nepal for those who are confident of their fitness.

LODGE TREKS

Centuries of trading throughout the mountains of Nepal have produced an excellent network of footpaths, along which village inns or lodges supply food and overnight accommodation for local travellers. With the advent of trekking, many of these have learned to [6] _____ for western tastes as well. Some have simple [7] _____ bedrooms and [8] _____ local food, others offer more comfortable accommodation with quite sophisticated menus. These lodges provide an easy alternative to camping on trek, and on the more popular trails they can be a better option: cheaper and with an added human interest, they provide extra shelter and comfort, a greater variety of food, and village contacts. On the practical level they enable us to operate a trek with smaller [9] _____ so that we cause less impact on the villages we pass through. As you have a choice of menu we do not include food or drinks in the price, while still providing the guides and porters who are essential if you are to enjoy the scenery to the [10] _____.

Outline itinerary: Day 1 Depart London. **2/3** Arrive Kathmandu; sightseeing. **4** Drive to Besisahar. **5/21** Trekking. **22** Fly to Kathmandu. **23** Depart Kathmandu. **24** London.

Trekking profile: 17 days walking with full portelage; altitude maximum 5,316 m., average 2,800m. Grade C.

Group size: min.2, max.12.

Accommodation: 3 nights hotels, 18 nights lodges.

Food: Meals NOT included except breakfast in Kathmandu and Pokhora; allow £45.

B For each of the gaps 1–10 in the text above choose the correct word from the options a–d. The first one has been done for you.

1 a *known*   b called   c labelled   d told
2 a provide   b suggest   c offer   d show
3 a difference   b change   c alteration   d variety
4 a too   b enough   c so   d such
5 a opening   b beginning   c introduction d preface
6 a cater   b feed   c supply   d serve
7 a communist   b communal   c common   d communicative
8 a antique   b historic   c traditional   d classical
9 a numbers   b quantities   c amounts   d volumes
10 a whole   b all   c full   d complete

C A potential customer who has heard about the Nepal lodge treks is phoning you to ask for some more details. Using the information above, complete the extract from the conversation, remembering that you are trying to sell the holiday.

… so from that point of view it doesn't matter whether you go in the spring or autumn.

CUSTOMER   And the £1,175 – does that include everything?

TRAVEL AGENT   1 _____

CUSTOMER   And the trek starts in Kathmandu, presumably?

TRAVEL AGENT   2 _____

CUSTOMER   So how long does the trip last altogether?

TRAVEL AGENT   3 _____

CUSTOMER   So I'd need to take a month off, really. How many people are there in a group?

TRAVEL AGENT   4 _____

CUSTOMER   I see. What is special about the Annapurna circuit – I mean, how does it differ from some of the other treks?

TRAVEL AGENT   5 _____

CUSTOMER   Could you tell me a bit about accommodation – is it a camping trek?

TRAVEL AGENT   6 _____

CUSTOMER   I see. And what are they really like? Are they quite comfortable?

TRAVEL AGENT   7 _____

CUSTOMER   I see. Now, as I said a moment ago, this is all new to me and I just want to be sure that I'm going to be able to manage the trek – I mean, how difficult is it?

TRAVEL AGENT   8 _____

CUSTOMER   Yes, I would say I am. I go jogging once or twice a week, play squash, that sort of thing.

TRAVEL AGENT   9 _____

CUSTOMER   OK, well, that sounds very interesting.

TRAVEL AGENT   10 _____

CUSTOMER   Yes, that would be great. My address is 17 Lawson Avenue …

12

Developments in tourism

1 Reading   **A Japanese space hotel**

A Below is an article about a Japanese space hotel. Some of the sentences have been removed from the text. Read the article and then look at **B**.

SPACE HOTEL

'*Thank you for travelling with British Airways' new Orbitours service. We are cruising at about 25,000 kph at an altitude of ninety km, and have almost left the Earth's atmosphere. In a few minutes we will start the docking manoeuvre with the Tokyo Orbital international hotel…*'

Japan's Shimuzu Corporation is already making plans for the day that there are regular flights into space, not for astronauts and cosmonauts, but for tourists and sightseers.

The company expects that, within thirty years, space will provide a vast new frontier for the adventurous. [1] *c*

The elderly will enjoy a low-gravity environment, where sleep is more comfortable than on earth. Honeymooners will find that microgravity adds extra excitement to their first night together. [2] ___

As the aerospaceplane closes in on Tokyo Orbital International, passengers will witness a hotel that looks quite unlike any on earth. Various sections will be connected to a central shaft, like meat on a skewer. At the bottom of this cosmic shish-kebab will be the docking port. [3] ___

Within them, the air will be cleaned by single-celled plants called algae, and artificial gravity will be created by rotating the wheel at about three times a minute.

Though it is only seventy per cent of the earth's pull, the artificial gravity will allow conventional hotel room fittings such as flush lavatories, showers, and wash basins. The space tourist will enjoy luxury that will be a far cry from the capsule hotels currently enjoyed by Japanese businessmen. [4] ___

Three million kilograms of junk are estimated to swarm within 2,000 kilometres of earth. A piece just a few centimetres in diameter could destroy a module on the hotel, so special measures will be required to protect tourists.

The intrepid tourist may also suffer from a close relative of sea sickness – space adaptation syndrome. [5] ___

Space tourism will not come cheap – estimates of the cost abound, ranging from tens of thousands to millions of dollars, depending on the trip, time-scale, available technology, and the market for the experience. [6] ___

As for whether space tourism will occur at all, we can look at the development of air travel. [7] ___

If this pattern is repeated in space, there are bound to be commercial flights within the next sixty years.

B The following sentences have been removed from the text. Read them through and put them in the correct place. The first one has been done for you.

a Above it there will be an inverted pyramid holding the hotel lounge, and at the top there will be sixty-four separate rooms arranged in modules around the edge of a vast eighty-metre diameter wheel.

b Some technical consultants estimate that the cost per seat could fall from $4 million in the space shuttle to $10,000 in a 'spacebus'.

c *Then anyone with enough money will be able to experience the thrill of space flight, from the push of high g-forces on take-off, to the moment when the sky changes from blue into the pitch black of space.*

d In the past sixty years the number of people who cross the Atlantic has grown from a handful of daredevils to some 25 million a year.

e Around half of those who have gone into space suffer this unpleasant side-effect, though effective drugs are likely to be available in the future to overcome the nausea and discomfort.

f Several hazards face the space traveller, however.

g And under the flashing strobes of the low-gravity discotheque, a new generation of bizarre dance styles will evolve.

C Are the following statements true (T) or false (F)?

1 The Shimuzu Corporation has started building the first space hotel.
2 The company expects that cheap space travel will be a reality within thirty years.
3 The space hotel is likely to appeal to different age groups.
4 The hotel lounge will be beneath the rooms.
5 The hotel will create its own gravity by spinning slowly.
6 Hotel guests will still be able to use facilities such as toilets.
7 The hotel will run the risk of being hit by pieces of debris in space.
8 About fifty per cent of today's astronauts suffer from sea sickness.
9 Most experts agree on what the likely price of space travel will be.
10 Space travel will expand as rapidly as air travel.

2   **Making predictions**

Read the following statements. Show to what extent you agree or disagree by giving each statement a number between 1 and 5.

In the next fifty years...

	Yes		Maybe		No
	1	2	3	4	5
❶ People will be able to stay in space hotels.					
❷ High air travel costs will make mass tourism a thing of the past.					
❸ Computers will make it unnecessary to learn languages.					
❹ Belgium will become a major international tourist destination.					
❺ Beach holidays in the Mediterranean will become less popular.					
❻ New forms of transport will be invented.					
❼ Passports will be abolished.					
❽ Most travel agents will work from home.					

Possibilities and probabilities

Look at the way we use the following words and phrases to talk about how probable a future event is.

Definite	Passports **will definitely** be abolished.
	Passports **are bound to** be abolished.
Likely	Passports **will probably** be abolished.
	Passports **are likely to** be abolished.
Possible	Passports **may/might** be abolished.
Unlikely	Passports **probably won't** be abolished.
	Passports **are unlikely to** be abolished.
Impossible	Passports **certainly won't** be abolished.
	Passports **definitely won't** be abolished.

Write short paragraphs about four of the topics in exercise 2, using the language above and giving reasons for your opinion. One has been done for you.

1 *People will probably be able to stay in space hotels, but there are unlikely to be very many of them. They will cost a great deal, and will therefore be expensive to stay in.*

2 _____
_____

3 _____
_____

4 _____
_____

5 _____
_____

Talking about mistakes

A Look at the following sentence. It talks about something that happened in the past and about its result.

Our flight to Cairo was delayed. As a result, we missed our connecting flight to Nairobi.

If we want to imagine a different past situation and a different result, we need to use the third conditional. We can rephrase the sentence as follows:

If + past perfect (*had done*)   *would have* + past participle (*done*)

If our flight to Cairo had been on time, we wouldn't have missed our connecting flight to Nairobi.

B Rephrase the following sentences using the third conditional. The first one has been done for you.

1 The developers built so many hotels that they ruined the resort.

   If the developers hadn't built so many hotels, they wouldn't have ruined the resort.

2 The weather was so bad that we didn't enjoy our holiday.

   If ... _____

3 Our brochures arrived late. We lost a lot of customers.

   If ... _____

4 He didn't have any travel insurance. He had to pay the hospital bill himself.

   If ... _____

5 You didn't reconfirm your ticket. We didn't book you a seat on the flight.

   If ... _____

6 You didn't discuss the problem with the representative. She didn't sort it out.

   If ... _____

5   Mistakes and missed opportunities

Look at the pictures showing mistakes that have been made. Read the notes and for each set of pictures, say what should or should not have happened and what the alternative was. The first one has been done for you

1 The mistake: to build so many high rise hotels
The missed opportunity: to plan the development more carefully/not spoil the resort

They shouldn't have built so many high rise hotels. If they had planned the development more carefully, they wouldn't have spoiled the resort.

2 The mistake: to allow hotels to employ foreigners
The missed opportunity: to insist on hiring local staff/unemployment go down

_____

3 The mistake: not to control the fishing industry
The missed opportunity: to limit catches/preserve fish stocks

_____

4 The mistake: to let the hotels use so much water
The missed opportunity: to control water supply/protect the local farmers

_____

5 The mistake: to allow foreign companies into the country
The missed opportunity: to keep them out/enable local hotels to succeed

_____

6   Vocabulary   Tourism and the environment

Complete the sentences using a word from column **A** and a word from column **B**. The first one has been done for you.

A		B	
air	local	disposal	layer
developing	ozone	pollution	*country*
endangered	waste	friendly	species
environmentally	water	materials	conservation

1 If you visit a <u>developing</u> <u>country</u> such as Bangladesh or Nepal, try to eat and drink local produce.

2 Avoid using areosol sprays which contain CFCs that damage the _____ _____ .

3 Never buy ivory, tiger skins, or any other products that come from _____ _____ .

4 By travelling on public transport, you are not adding to _____ _____ .

5 If you take shampoo and sun creams make sure they are _____ _____ and can be recycled.

6 Make sure your hotel has a green _____ _____ policy and does not dump everything into the sea.

7 You can help with _____ _____ by taking showers rather than baths.

8 Make sure your souvenirs are made from _____ _____ and are not imported.

A Below is an article about the environmental policies of the tour operator Exodus. Some of the words have been removed from the text. Read the article and choose the correct words from the box below to fill in the spaces. The first one has been done for you.

individual   recruited   retain   *effects*   dispose   expense   in   blend
respect   offering   upon   interest   sound   character   cope   rather

12

Developments in tourism

Our environmental policy

At EXODUS, we are very well aware of the potential ¹ *effects* of tourism on remote places and small, simple communities. It is our firm belief that our small-group philosophy provides an environmentally ² _____ approach that increases the positive effects and keeps the negative ones to a minimum.

Our type of holidays – organized by, led by, and bought by people who are genuinely interested ³ _____ and sympathetic towards the environment and culture that they are visiting – are undoubtedly responsible tourism, ⁴ _____ more enjoyable holidays and helping host nations preserve and protect the very reasons why we visit them. In particular, we believe that the following are the key points in this philosophy.

Small groups

A small group makes our impact ⁵ _____ communities and cultures both minimal and positive: a village can ⁶ _____ with a dozen people, but a coach load will often swamp it.

Accommodation

Where it's possible, we like to use accommodation with a local ⁷ _____ – not just because it's more interesting, but because it's more beneficial too. Our tourist and first class hotels are often locally owned ⁸ _____ than multinational, and we often use small family run accommodation, providing a direct local benefit.

Food

When staying in hotels, we generally leave the choice of a venue for most main meals to the ⁹ _____, which not only gives you more choice, but it spreads the potential local benefit too.

When we are camping, we try to purchase as much fresh food as is practical locally – another two-sided benefit. When we leave a site we ¹⁰ _____ of our rubbish and leave the area as we would wish to find it.

Local staff

Wherever practical, our guides, porters, and means of transport are ¹¹ _____ locally, in order to benefit the local people directly. We are also careful to ensure that local staff and agents receive a fair rate for their work; we never try to minimize our prices at the ¹² _____ of local collaborators.

Our own staff

We encourage our own staff to take an active ¹³ _____ in the environment and ecology of the places that they visit, and to advise and assist groups to ¹⁴ _____ in with and respect the communities they meet.

Ecotourism – the way forward

Ecotourism may be a trendy new term, but it refers to something that we at EXODUS have been doing for years. The key element is ¹⁵ _____ for the people and places that we visit, so that they benefit from our presence and are able to ¹⁶ _____ their cultural integrity for future generations.

EX OD US

Word and preposition combinations

In the text above there were a number of word and preposition combinations (*dispose of*, *interested in*, *respect for*, etc.). Complete the puzzle by finding the missing words from the sentences and filling them in. The first one has been done for you.

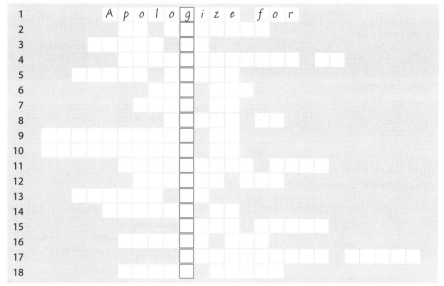

1 Ladies and gentlemen, we ___ ___ the delay, but expect we will be able to take off soon.

2 I'm afraid Mr Nelson won't be back till next Monday. He is away ___ ___ for two weeks.

3 At Exodus, we are fully ___ ___ the need to take care of the environment.

4 One ___ ___ staying in a space hotel is that it can make you feel ill.

5 One of the hotel guests was very ___ ___ the noise outside her room during the night.

6 Take a little local currency in case you need to ___ ___ a taxi or a snack.

7 This year there has been a sharp ___ ___ the number of tourists, so the hotels are full.

8 Air accident investigators are looking into the ___ ___ the crash.

9 On the first evening all our guests at the resort get an ___ ___ a drinks party in a local restaurant.

10 If you're ___ ___ art, you might like to consider the holidays we arrange in Florence.

11 If you are not absolutely ___ ___ your holiday, we will give you your money back.

12 The city of Paris is ___ ___ its excellent restaurants and sophisticated night life.

13 There are always a few passengers on every flight who are ___ ___ flying.

14 The journey usually takes about an hour, but it does ___ ___ the traffic.

15 Don't worry – if your daughter is under twelve, we will assign a stewardess to ___ ___ her.

16 I am sure we have paid them – I sent them a ___ ___ fifty pounds last Monday.

17 The tour operator received a number of ___ ___ the poor facilities at the hotel.

18 You needn't book the holiday now – you can go home and ___ ___ it if you like.

Answer key

Answer key

Unit 1 (p 4)   The history and development of tourism

1 Sights and cities
1 *Eiffel Tower, Paris*   2 Acropolis, Athens
3 Big Ben, London   4 Statue of Liberty, New York
5 Opera House, Sydney   6 Colosseum, Rome

2 Likes and dislikes
A 1 *She loves travelling abroad.*
    2 She loves meeting new people.
    3 She is interested in ancient Egypt.
    4 She dislikes going on cruises.
    5 She doesn't mind flying.
    6 She hates really long flights.
B No set answer

3 Simple past and present perfect
A 1 Correct.
    2 My brother *has been* in England since July.
    3 Manuel *finished* his diploma in tourism last year.
    4 Correct.
    5 The agent says she *sent* you the tickets yesterday.
    6 … she's been with Qantas *since* last May.
    7 Correct.
    8 My father *learned* a little English when he was at school.
    9 Correct.
   10 I have worked for Jaybee Travel *for* two years.
   11 The flight *hasn't arrived* yet.
B 1 *Have you ever worked*   2 I have had
    3 I worked   4 I was
    5 did you enjoy it   6 I loved it
    7 it was   8 I went
    9 they have given   10 have you applied
   11 I have only just sent off   12 I haven't received
   13 I have always thought   14 I decided

4 Vocabulary   Tourism and travel
A **Money**
insurance policy, price war, traveller's cheques, currency, foreign exchange
People and jobs
travel agent, passenger, tour guide, tourist
Tourist attractions
art gallery, museum, sightseeing, excursion, beach
Air travel
airline, check-in desk, in-flight magazine, departure lounge, boarding card, charter flight, plane
Other transport
railway, road, train, stagecoach
B No set answers

5 Reading   Around the world in 222 days
A 1F, 2F, 3T, 4T, 5T, 6T, 7T, 8F
B **Itinerary**
    1 *Liverpool*   2 New York   3 Japan
    4 Shanghai   5 Singapore   6 Bay of Bengal
    7 Benares   8 Bombay   9 Red Sea
   10 Cairo   11 England

6 Simple present active or passive
1 *are held*   2 want   3 eat
4 arrives   5 are sung   6 pushes
7 are attached   8 pull   9 is called
10 are organized   11 walk   12 are not harmed
13 heal   14 takes   15 are situated
16 be arranged

7 Writing   Describing a festival
No set answer

---

8 Review
1 *Laker Airways was founded in 1966.*
2 The first Olympics were held in 776 BC.
3 César Manrique was born in Arrecife.
4 The Suez Canal was opened in 1869.
5 The first package tours were organized by Thomas Cook.
6 The Jardin de Cactus was designed by César Manrique.
7 The Pyramids were built by the Ancient Egyptians.
8 The Mona Lisa was painted by Leonardo da Vinci.

Unit 2 (p 10)   The organization and structure of tourism

1 Question forms
1 *How did you travel to the airport?*
2 How long did you have to wait to check in?
3 Did you have any problems finding your way around?
4 Which/What airline are you flying with?
5 Where are you going?
6 Are you travelling on business or on holiday?
7 Have you used the duty-free shop?
8 What other airport facilities have you used/did you use?
9 Are there any improvements (that) you would like to see?

2 Indirect questions
1 *Could you tell me which hotel you will be staying at?*
2 May I ask if you have ever been there before?
3 Can you tell me if anyone recommended it to you?
4 Would you mind telling me why you chose it?
5 Could you tell me how much it costs?
6 Can you tell me what facilities it has?
7 May I ask if the hotel has a courtesy bus?
8 Would you mind telling me when you will be leaving?

3 The language of graphs

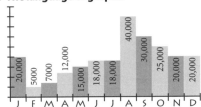

4 Charts and statistics

5 Vocabulary   Jobs in tourism

1 c u r a t o r
2 p o r t e r
3 c o n t r o l l e r
4 c u s t o m s
5 p i l o t
6 s t e w a r d e s s
7 g u a r d
8 b a g g a g e
9 c h a m b e r m a i d

6 Vocabulary   Sectors of the tourism industry
A&B No set answers

7 Becoming a flight attendant
1h, 2b, 3e, 4c, 5a, 6g, 7d, 8f

Unit 3 (p 16)   Travel agents

1 Vocabulary   Holiday types
A **Skiing**   slopes, snow, medical insurance
    Safari   lodge, warden, wildlife
    Cruise   cabin, steward, port
    Package   beach, hotel, charter flight
    Fly-drive   flight, car-hire, route maps
    Self-catering   cooker, fridge, freezer
    Backpacking   hitch-hiking, coach, hostel
    Adventure   white-water rafting, canoeing, mountaineering
B No set answers

2 Taking a booking
_3_ JANE That's right. How can I help you, sir?
_1_ JANE Good morning. This is Star Travel. Jane speaking.
_15_ JANE Goodbye.
_13_ JANE Certainly. I'll just give you the booking reference number. It's LF2254G.
_9_ JANE It leaves at 6.30 and arrives at 8.00. Would that suit you?
_5_ JANE I'm not sure. I'll check availability for you. Do you have a preference for any airline?
_11_ JANE Do you want to confirm it?
_7_ JANE OK. Now, let me see … there's availability on the 18th on an early morning flight with Lufthansa.
_10_ ALAN Yes, that would be fine.
_6_ ALAN I'd prefer British Airways or Lufthansa.
_12_ ALAN Yes, please, and could you charge it to our account?
_8_ ALAN How early?
_2_ ALAN Hello, this is Alan March from GKC. I believe we have an account with you.
_4_ ALAN I'd like to book a flight to Munich on the 18th of November. Do you think there will be any seats left?
_14_ ALAN LF2254G. OK, thanks very much. Goodbye.

3 Making suggestions
Sample answers only
1 *Have you thought of going by ferry? It's very comfortable and there are lots of different sailings.*
2 Why don't you hire a car? They're very good value and you can book in advance.
3 Have you thought of getting her an Inter-rail card? They are valid for a month and she can go wherever she likes.
4 Why don't you stay at the Sheraton? It's five minutes from Terminal 2 and there's a free courtesy bus.
5 How about going in spring? The weather's lovely and it's not too crowded.
6 You could go to Disneyland® Paris. It's easy to reach and it's very popular with children.
7 If I were you I'd take the bus tour – it's very interesting and it only lasts two hours.

4 Vocabulary   Business travel
1 *limousine service*   2 express check-in
3 automatic upgrade   4 extra leg-room
5 incentive scheme   6 mini-bar
7 modem point   8 fax machine
9 meeting rooms   10 conference hall
11 corporate discount

5 Obligation and necessity
Sample answers only
1 *You aren't allowed to park here.*
2 You have to keep your luggage with you all the time.
3 You don't have to get a visa.
4 You can bring in 200 cigarettes.
5 You're allowed to smoke here.
6 You aren't allowed to get a job.
7 You have to pay the rest by the end of the month.
8 You can't give the ticket to anyone else.

6 Telephone language
1 *put*   2 calling   3 this is
4 busy   5 hold   6 ringing
7 speaking   8 afraid   9 leave
10 catch   11 line   12 repeat
13 get   14 has   15 gets

7 Reading   Virgin Freeway

1T, 2T, 3F, 4T, 5T, 6F, 7T, 8F, 9T, 10T

8 Dialogue completion

1 *Yes, it's an air miles scheme run by Virgin, and you collect points or air miles every time you fly, and you can use them to get free flights depending on how many air miles you've collected.*

2 No, not at all – there are a number of other airlines you can get points from – for example, British Midland and SAS.

3 All sorts of things, like free flights, holidays, meals out, and so on.

4 No, because you only get points when you've done a certain number of flights.

5 You'd get double the number of points, which would be enough for a couple of flights to Europe.

6 No, you can get them from some petrol stations, hotels, and so on.

7 No, you have to book at least three weeks in advance.

8 Yes, that would be fine.

9 You can do it by phone – I'll give you the number. It's 0171 924 9105.

Unit 4 (p 22)   Tour operation

1 Travel agents and tour operators

A 1a, 2b, 3a, 4b, 5b, 6a, 7b, 8b

B

		C	o	n	t	r	a	c	t	
1		C	o	n	t	r	a	c	t	
2	m	a	n	i	f	e	s	t		
3		r	a	c	k	s				
4		r	o	o	m	i	n	g		
5	d	i	s	c	o	u	n	t		
6	n	e	g	o	t	i	a	t	i	n	g
7	v	o	u	c	h	e	r			
8	b	r	o	c	h	u	r	e	s		

2 Reading   Types of message

A&B 1 Space b   2 Space c   3 Space d
    4 Space e   5 Space a

C 1 The first message was the *letter* from Terry Harvey to Jack Jones.

2 The second message was the fax from C. Kostas to Terry Harvey.

3 The third message was the phone message from Terry Harvey to Jack Jones.

4 The fourth message was the e-mail from Jack Jones to Lee.

3 Setting up negotiations

1	*ought to*	2	idea	3	about
4	convenient	5	could	6	say
7	bring	8	might	9	agree
10	understand	11	anything else	12	honest
13	look forward to				

4 Preliminary negotiations

Sample answers only

1 That's not very convenient for me. Could you make Friday at 11.00?

2 Yes, I thought we ought to talk about how many rooms we will need for next season, and I think we could look at prices, but we don't need to sort that out now.

3 Yes, I think that would be a good idea. It might be useful if I bring along some letters to look at.

4 I see your point, but I can't really go along with that. I suggest that we look at other alternatives, such as booking more rooms.

5 Yes, there is. I'd like to bring up the question of cancellation charges. To be honest, we felt they were far too high last year.

6 That's fine. I'll see you on Friday at 11.00.

5 Responding to complaints

A a2, b4, c1, d5, e3

B Most helpful: 5, 4, 2, 3   Least helpful: 1

C **Sample answers only**

1 I'm so sorry to hear that. I'll get the doctor to come and have a look at her.

2 I'm very sorry. I'll see if we can get you moved to another room.

3 I am very sorry – the pump is being repaired at the moment, but we're hoping to get the pool working again as soon as we can.

4 I'm very sorry. I'll sort it out immediately.

5 I'm sorry to hear that. I'll have a word with the chef and see if he can come up with anything more to your liking.

6 Answering a letter of complaint

A 1F, 2T, 3T, 4F, 5T, 6F

B No set answers

Unit 5 (p 28)   Air Travel

1 Vocabulary   At the airport

1	terminal building	2	check-in desk
3	economy class	4	boarding card
5	conveyor belt	6	hand luggage
7	excess baggage	8	departure lounge
9	passport control	10	departure gate

2 Talking about procedures

A	1	b first of all	2	a immediately
	3	b at the same time	4	b the last stage
	5	b as soon as	6	b then
	7	c beforehand	8	b simultaneously
	9	b the last stage	10	a finally

B No set answers

3 Vocabulary   Air travel

A **Areas inside a plane**
aisle, flight deck, galley

Staff
cabin crew, co-pilot, navigator, pilot

Safety equipment
life-jacket, oxygen mask, *seat-belt*, whistle

Parts of an aircraft
landing gear, tail, nose, wing

4 Writing   Seating arrangements

A	Row 1	window	Anna Mason
		centre	Mrs Jones + infant
		aisle	Mr Jones
	Row 2	window	Jack Winters
		centre	Mary Watson
		aisle	Helen Hamblin

B No set answers

5 Giving directions

A 1 *meeting point*   2 bureau de change
  3 post box

B 1 *duty-free shop*   2 hotel reservations
  3 bureau de change

C 1 As you come out of the souvenir shop, the children's playroom is opposite you, between the men's toilets and the video room.

2 Go straight ahead through customs and out on to the arrivals concourse. The car-hire desk is on your left between the information desk and hotel reservations.

6 Writing   International executive lounge club

No set answer

7 Reading   Want to join the jet set?

1F, 2F, 3F, 4T, 5T, 6T, 7F, 8T, 9T, 10F

Unit 6 (p 34)   Travel by sea and river – cruises and ferries

1 Reading   Information about a cruise

A&B 1d, 2h, 3g, 4i, 5k, 6f, 7c, 8b, 9e, 10j, 11a

2 Passive tense review

A a The ship has been completely modernized.
The restaurants have been extensively redecorated.
A fitness centre has been opened on Deck C.
We have also built a new pool on the upper deck.

b Breakfast is served daily from 7-11.
The main restaurants open at midday and close at 12.30.

We offer 24-hour room service.
Please note a small charge is made for this.

c You will have the chance to go ashore for shopping or sightseeing.
Passengers will be taken to the port by speedboat.
You will be collected at 6.30 p.m.
We will set sail again at 9.00.

d One of the passengers got held up during a shore visit.
As a result, he was left behind.
We had to set sail without him.
Fortunately he was picked up at the next port of call.

B **Sample answer only**

1 Ladies and gentlemen, welcome aboard the *Ramada Diamond* and to our cruise of the Caribbean. If you have sailed with us before, you will notice that the ship *has been completely modernized.*
The restaurants have been extensively redecorated and a new fitness centre has been opened on Deck C. We have also built a beautiful new pool on the upper deck, which we are sure you will enjoy.

2 We sincerely hope that you will enjoy the gourmet food we provide and would like to remind you of mealtimes in the main restaurants. Breakfast is served daily from 7 to 11. The main restaurants open at midday and close just after midnight, at 12.30. We also offer 24 hour room service, but please note that a small charge is made for this.

3 Our first port of call will be St Lucia on Wednesday. You will have the chance to go ashore and to go shopping or sightseeing. Passengers will be taken to the port by speedboat, and you will be collected at 6.30 p.m.

4 Please note: may we remind you of the importance of pick-up times, as there was an unfortunate incident on one of our recent cruises. One of the passengers got held up during a shore visit, and as a result, he was left behind and we had to set sail without him. Furtunately he was picked up at the next port of call. We trust that this will not happen to you and hope you have an enjoyable cruise.

C 1 *The ship was still being redecorated.*

2 The cabins were still being painted.

3 Only one of the restaurants had been opened.

4 The start of the cruise was not delayed.

5 They were not told about the problems.

6 Passengers are usually compensated for this sort of thing.

7 The company will definitely be fined.

3 Issuing tickets

1	some	2	the day after tomorrow.
3	except	4	to	5	are
6	fare	7	single	8	advance
9	board	10	takes		

4 Forms of the future

A 1 will give – arrive   2 will take – arrives
  3 will give – leaves   4 will contact – confirm
  5 get – will visit

B 1 are going to   2 will
  3 am going to   4 am going to
  5 will

C **Itineraries**
You're arriving in St Vincent on Monday; you're spending the day there and the yacht sets sail at 6.00 in the evening. On Tuesday, you're travelling to Bequia, and you'll have the chance to visit the whaling museum. On Wednesday you're spending the day in Mustique, and you're having lunch at Charleston Bay. On Thursday you're going to Palm Island, where you'll have the chance to go scuba diving. On Friday you're crossing to Union Island, and you catch the 6.25 flight to St Lucia. You're flying back on Saturday, and you arrive back at 18.30.

5 International etiquette

No set answer

6 Vocabulary   Hotels and cruise ships

1 *chain*
2 double rooms
3 window
4 floor
5 room service
6 check in
7 staff
8 guests
9 check out
10 fleet
11 two-berth cabins
12 porthole
13 deck
14 cabin service
15 embark
16 crew
17 passengers
18 disembark

7 Writing   A cruise ship
No set answer

Unit 7 (p 40)   Travel by road and rail

1 Talking about preferences
Sample answers only
1 *I'd rather work for a big travel agency than for myself because I'd be able to learn more about the business, and then maybe I might like to start my own company.*
2 I prefer trains because they're faster and you can get up and walk around.
3 I'd prefer to stay in a city because there's much more to do.
4 I prefer travelling by car because you can go where you want when you want.
5 I'd rather have a rail pass because the trains would be more comfortable.

2 Vocabulary   Road and rail travel

1	2	3
compartment	track	keys
4	5	6
steam	map	platform
7	8	9
mileage	energetic	couchette
10	11	12
engine	exit	tachograph
13	14	15
hotel	luggage locker	restaurant car
16	17	18
return ticket	taxi cab	buffet
19	20	21
tunnel	limousine	escalator
22	23	24
refreshments	sleeper	rail pass

3 Comparing and contrasting
A 1 *Even though the coach to Madrid was very cheap, I don't think we'd do that journey again.*
2 Not only do you get cheaper travel with a rail pass, but you also get discounts in hotels.
3 If you travel in low season, it's usually much cheaper; what's more, you avoid the crowds.
4 Even though there wasn't much snow, we had a really good skiing holiday.
5 She had a great time travelling round Europe, in spite of the weather.
6 Suzi Cars only hire out small cars, whereas Hertz have a full range of vehicles.
7 Although the flight time from London to Paris is short, it can take ages to get to and from the airport.
8 On the one hand, the ferries are very regular; on the other hand, they are very slow.
B 1 *We managed to arrive on time in spite of the heavy traffic.*
2 Not only was the coach driver incompetent, but he was rude as well.
3 Intercity trains are very fast, whereas local trains are not.
4 We arrived in good shape although the journey was/had been long.
5 In spite of the good discount, my air pass was very expensive.
6 Not only is the coach fully air-conditioned, but it also has an excellent video system.

4 Adjectives
A *beautiful* wonderful helpful
comfortable hospitable enjoyable
dirty friendly noisy
energetic panoramic romantic
famous luxurious delicious
national traditional typical
B **Sample answer only**
The Northern Express will take you from Kuala Lumpur's *famous* railway station all the way to the *romantic* city of Bangkok. If you travel first class you will have the pleasure of staying in a *luxurious* compartment with *comfortable* furniture, and our *helpful* staff will be on hand to help you with anything you need. The Northern Express also has a *wonderful* restaurant that serves *delicious* food, and as you look out, you will be able to enjoy *panoramic* views of the *beautiful* countryside of Malaysia and Thailand.

5 Giving advice
Sample answers only
1 Yes, I think it would be quite good for you. Although it's on quite a noisy road, it has lots of rooms and a big garden.
2 I don't think that would be a good idea. Although the overnight coach is cheap, it's very tiring, and there are better alternatives.
3 That's an excellent idea; although it's quite expensive, you can save a lot and go anywhere.
4 That's not a good idea. Although the weather is fine in August, Venice is very crowded and it would be difficult to find accommodation.

6 Dealing with problems
Sample answers only
1 There's nothing to worry about. I'll phone the airport and see if your bags are there.
2 There's nothing to worry about. I'll send someone up to get rid of it immediately.
3 Calm down. Just take it easy and you'll soon get the hang of it.
4 Don't worry – I can contact the Embassy and if we need to, we can get you a new one.
5 Please try and stay calm. I'll get a doctor to come up to the room right away.
6 Don't worry – if you do miss the flight, you can get on another one a little later on.

7 Negative prefixes
A uncomfortable
unpleasant
unacceptable
illegal
illegible
illiterate
discourteous
dishonest
disorganized
impractical
impolite
impatient
irrational
irregular
irrelevant
inaccurate
incompetent
incapable
B 1 *illegal*
2 disorganized
3 uncomfortable
4 inaccurate
5 irrelevant
6 impractical

8 Writing   Problems on a coach tour
No set answer

Unit 8 (p 46)   Tickets, reservations, and insurance

1 Vocabulary   Numbers
1 a *eighteen twenty-five*
  b eighteen point two five per cent
2 a six seven one six seven four five
  b six million seven hundred and sixteen thousand seven hundred and forty-five
3 a four point nine nine
  b four (pounds) ninety-nine
4 a nineteen ninety seven
  b one thousand nine hundred and ninety-seven kilometres
5 a twenty-eight degrees centigrade
  b twenty-eight per cent
6 a seven forty-five
  b seven point four five
7 a six point four five two
  b six thousand four hundred and fifty-two

2 Describing facilities
1 *tropical*
2 luxurious
3 finest
4 garden
5 endless
6 speciality
7 idyllic
8 varied
9 fine
10 ideal

3 Explaining pricing
1 Well, let's have a look. The basic price, between the 29th of March and the 12th of April, is £1,169 per person. For two people that's £2,338. Then the half board costs £24.80 per person times two, which is £49.60 per night. That times twelve comes to £595.20. So the basic price plus the cost of half board comes to a total of £2,933.20 per person.
2 Well, let's have a look. The basic price for nineteen nights in May is £1,195. Then you need to add the single room supplement of £32 per night. That times nineteen comes to £608. Bed and breakfast is £9.80, which, times nineteen, comes to £186.20. So the total price of your holiday would come to £1,989.20.

4 Dates and figures
1 *18th*
2 £1,189
3 include
4 £24.80
5 come
6 £2,378
7 times
8 £49.60
9 twelve
10 £595.20
11 plus
12 £2,973.20
13 17th
14 £939
15 5th
16 special offer
17 November
18 December
19 discount
20 £93
21 minus
22 £846
23 total
24 £1,692

5 Flight information on the Internet
A Departing from: London
  Arriving at: Nairobi
  Departing from: London Are Airports, GB
  Arriving at: Jomo Kenyatta Intl, KE
  Leaving on: Month: September
      Day: 21
  Number of persons: 2
C *No, there aren't. The only direct flight leaves on the 22nd and gets in at 06.55 on the 23rd.*
1 That's with Kenya Airways.
2 No, I'm afraid not. There's only availability in Economy.
3 You could fly to Schipol and then go to Jeddah, change at Jeddah and fly to Nairobi.
4 A couple of hours – just under.
5 Let's have a look – about seven hours.
6 There are seats in Business Class to Schipol, but the flights to Jeddah and to Nairobi would have to be First Class.
7 Yes, you can go via Schipol again and then change at Cairo.
8 An hour and a quarter at Schipol and two hours at Cairo.
9 14.20.
10 Yes, there are.
11 There's not much in it – five minutes. The Cairo flight gets in at 06.30 on the 22nd and the Jeddah flight gets in at 06.25.

6 Describing events in the past
A 1 *took*
2 was having
3 passed
4 was behaving
5 was holding
6 got
7 knew
8 had been
9 was lying
10 had been stolen
11 was looking
12 realized
13 had bought
B No set answers

7 Writing   An accident
No set answers

Unit 9 (p 52)   Tourist information

1 Vocabulary   Tourist attractions and facilities
A 1 *cathedral*
2 art gallery
3 fortress
4 theme
5 flea market
6 theatre
7 restaurant
8 night club
B Moscow

2 Additional information clauses

1 which   2 who   3 which   4 when
5 whose   6 when   7 where

3 Tourist attractions in New Orleans

1 *The Confederate museum, which was built in 1891, is the oldest museum in Louisiana.*
2 The museum has a large art gallery, where you can see pictures of the Civil War.
3 Included in the collection are the personal effects of General Robert E. Lee, who was the leader of the Confederate army.
4 Destrehane plantation, which is the oldest in Louisiana, is conveniently located near the city.
5 It was originally built by the d'Estrehan family, who were French aristocrats.
6 It's a great place to visit in November, when the annual festival is held.
7 Longue Vue House, which is set in eight acres of beautiful countryside, is a beautiful English-style country home.
8 It originally belonged to the Stern family, whose collection of modern art is still housed there.
9 The estate has beautiful gardens, where you can have picnics and relax.

4 Tourist attractions in Canberra

Theatre

___all___ The Canberra Theatre Centre, in the heart of the city, provides performances *all* throughout the year. There are many other theatre venues
___side___ and, depending on the season, outdoor *side* performances and street theatre as well. For
___being___ details of what's *being* on during your stay, check the entertainment section of Thursday's *Canberra Times*.

Cinema

___have___ There are also *have* seven cinema complexes. At the Electric Shadows cinema in the city, you can catch up on classics and the latest movies.
___to___ If you're a film buff, you mustn't *to* miss the chance of browsing in their bookshop – it's
___most___ one of the *most* best in the country.

Clubs

___to___ For an inexpensive night out, visit *to* one of our licensed clubs. The facilities include
___an___ restaurants and bars offering *an* excellent value for money. Casino Canberra is a
___it___ European-style 'boutique' casino – which *it* means it's small enough to give you excellent
___for___ service, and big enough *for* to offer world-class facilities. Whether you're a first-timer or a high-roller, the friendly staff will make sure
___the___ you feel at *the* home.

5 Writing   Tourist attractions in your area

No set answers

6 Hotel facilities

1 As its name suggests, the Emerald Beach Hotel is situated right next to the beach.
2 How many of you are going?
3 And how old are the children?
4 Would you want to share a room?
5 Would you be interested in a room with a kitchen?
6 And how long are you planning to stay?
7 Well, for your wife and yourself, the cost would be $525 dollars for a week. The accommodation for the baby is free, but you would have to pay $30 for the crib. For your other child, the cost is half the adult rate, that is $262 plus $30 for a bed. In total that would all come to $847.

7 Simple past active or passive

1 *was put*   2 ordered
3 was taken   4 passed
5 was made   6 built
7 worked   8 began
9 were defeated   10 ordered
11 was controlled   12 were removed
13 was infested   14 was estimated
15 was completed

8 Dimensions

A Great Pyramid, Channel Tunnel, Golden Gate Bridge, Panama Canal
B 1   Channel Tunnel
     wide, width, length
   2   Golden Gate Bridge
     high, length
   3   Great Pyramid
     height, long
   4   Panama Canal
     long, depth, deep, width

9 Reading   A job in a leisure attraction

A 1c, 2e, 3a, 4d, 5f, 6g. The extra sentence is b.
B 1 yes   2 no   3 yes   4 yes   5 yes
   6 yes   7 yes   8 no   9 no   10 yes

Unit 10 (p 58)   Guiding

1 Personal qualities

A **sample answer only**

approachable	a	*aggressive*	c
ambitious	b	well-informed	a
arrogant	c	attractive	a
assertive	b	confident	a
domineering	c	enthusiastic	a
friendly	a	highly intelligent	a
untrustworthy	c	patronizing	c
rude	c	shy	b

B **No set answers**

2 Telephone language

1c, 2g, 3a, 4b, 5e, 6h, 7f, 8i, 9d

3 Word formation

A 1 idyllic   2 celebration
   3 historic   4 luxurious
   5 relaxing   6 architecture
   7 wonderful   8 arrangements
   9 performance   10 finest
   11 shopping   12 unquestionably
   13 beautiful   14 optional
   15 arrival

B 1 *No, we'll be arriving at Milan, and then we'll take a coach to our hotel in Vicenza.*
   2 No, you'll have the chance to settle in and have dinner.
   3 Yes, it's famous for its Palladian architecture.
   4 No, they're in Verona.
   5 No, it's a very easy drive.
   6 On day three we'll be spending the morning there.
   7 If you like. There's an optional tour or you can go round by yourself.
   8 We won't be going back to Milan – although we arrive there, we'll be leaving from Venice.

4 Leaving messages

Sample answers only

1 *Hello, this is Janie Mitchell in Vicenza doing the opera tour. I'm afraid the name of the restaurant we're meant to be having lunch in tomorrow didn't come through on the fax you sent me. Could you let me know what it is and whether I need to confirm the reservation? You can call me at the hotel and leave a message or send a fax to the hotel on 0239 77 33 44. Thank you.*
2 Hello, this is Janie Mitchell in Vicenza doing the opera tour. I'm calling to check that the pick-up point will be at the hotel. Could you also let me know whether the driver taking us there will also be bringing us back? You can call me at the hotel and leave a message or send a fax to the hotel on 0239 77 33 44. Thank you.
3 Hello, this is Janie Mitchell in Vicenza doing the opera tour. I'm ringing to confirm the reservation for our party of thirty plus two tonight at 18.00. We have five vegetarians in the party. Could you call me at the hotel and leave a message or send a fax to the hotel on 0239 77 33 44? Thank you.
4 Hello, this is Janie Mitchell in Vicenza doing the opera tour. I'm calling to check that you will have the tickets for the *Cosi fan tutti* performance and that I can pick them up at the door. I expect to be there just after 7.30. Could call me at the hotel and leave a message or send a fax to the hotel on 0239 77 33 44? Thank you.

5 Adjectives ending in -ed and -ing

1 interesting   2 bored   3 fascinating
4 satisfied   5 confusing   6 surprising
7 annoying   8 distracting   9 relaxed
10 amusing   11 exhausting   12 tired

6 Strong and weak adjectives

A **Neutral adjectives**

interesting	nice	impressive	good
famous	old	elegant	attractive
bad	long		

Strong adjectives

fascinating	wonderful	terrible
appalling	brilliant	fantastic
magnificent	superb	

B 1 fascinating   2 elegant   3 terrifying
   4 very   5 very   6 impressive

7 Writing task   The Tower of London

B **Sample answers only**

1 We are now about to enter the 'Bloody Tower'. It is called this because of the deaths of two young princes, who were the sons of Edward IV, who died in 1483. They were kept in the tower by their uncle Richard, Duke of Gloucester, who later became King. He is thought to have murdered the princes, although the bodies were never found.
2 We are now entering the Jewel House, where the royal crowns and other treasures are on display. The greatest treasure is the Imperial State Crown, which is worn by the monarch on major state occasions. The crown is encrusted with 2,800 diamonds and is set with several historic gemstones.
3 We are now entering the Chapel of St John, which is one of the most beautiful buildings in England. It dates from 1080 and contains a perfect barrel vault. The vault is built of Caen stone and is extremely well-preserved.

Unit 11 (p 64)   Promotion and marketing in tourism

1 Great marketing disasters

A&B   a3, b2, c1, d4, e5

2 First and second conditionals

A 1 was not (or were not) – would be
   2 had – would spend   3 will mind – is
   4 will phone – come   5 were – would complain
   6 had – would be able   7 did – would apply
   8 have – will do

B **Sample answers only**

1 *I think a web site would be better – if we set one up we'll be able to reach customers all over the world, but if we just handed out leaflets we wouldn't get the right sort of customers.*
2 I think an ad in the paper would be better – people will see it and ring up, but if we did a poster campaign, it'd take much too long to organize.
3 I would suggest a sporting event. If we advertise there, we'll reach lots of young people. If we advertised in a theatre, the audience would probably be much older.
4 A TV campaign would be too expensive and wouldn't target local people. If we hand out leaflets in the street, people will be able to just go round the corner and have a look.

3 Adjectives

A *Flight*

night	pleasant	charter

Staff

friendly	efficient	polite

Villa

well-equipped	luxurious	modern

View

wonderful	magnificent	panoramic

Meal

delicious	gourmet	three-course

Holiday

adventure	package	skiing

Beach

| secluded | sandy | beautiful |

Weather

| warm | humid | beautiful |

B **Sample answers only**

1 *a skiing holiday*

guaranteed snow	lively nightclubs
exhilarating runs	traditional chalet
expert instruction	

2 *a safari*

natural habitat	breath-taking scenery
endangered species	game reserve
wild animals	

3 *a trekking holiday*

special deal	snow-capped mountains
youth hostel	awe-inspiring scenery
specialized guides	

4 *a package holiday*

wonderful beaches	lovely weather
great value	family fun
modern hotel	

4 Selling holidays

No set answers

5 Superlatives and ranking

A 1 *Christ Church is the largest college in Oxford.*
2 St Petersburg is the most beautiful city in Russia.
3 Thomas Cook is one of the most famous travel agencies in the world.
4 Chichen Itza is one of the most ancient sites in Central America.
5 Birmingham is the second biggest city in England.
6 Kanchenjunga is the third highest mountain in the world.
7 Dhaulagiri is the seventh highest peak in Nepal.

B **No set answers**

6 Reading   Specialist holidays

A&B 1 a *known*   2 c offer
3 d variety   4 b enough
5 c introduction   6 a cater
7 b communal   8 c traditional
9 a numbers   10 c full

C **Sample answers only**

1 Meals are not inclued in this price, except for breakfast in Kathmandu and Pokhara. Eating is very cheap, though. We recommend customers to set aside a sum of about £45 to cover all other meals.
2 Yes, that's right. There's a day sightseeing in Kathmandu before you are driven to Besisahar to begin trekking.
3 The trip lasts twenty-four days altogether.
4 The maximum group size is twelve, the minimum two.
5 Well, this trek takes you through virtually every type of scenery that Nepal has to offer. We take you through a constant variety of landscapes, ranging from the sub-tropical, through the alpine to an arid semi-desert, akin to Tibet.
6 No, this isn't a camping trek. Overnight accommodation is in village inns or lodges. We chose this option for our customers because not only is it cheap, but it is a way of establishing friendly village contacts and adding greater human interest to your holiday experience.
7 It depends on where you are. Some of these lodges have simple communal bedrooms, others offer more comfortable accommodation with quite sophisticated menus.
8 Well, it can be demanding. The trip includes seventeen days' walking. Would you say that you are fairly fit?
9 We do also provide, included in the price, the guides and the porters who are essential if you are to enjoy your trip to the full.
10 Would you like us to send you our brochure with further details?

Unit 12 (p 70)   Developments in tourism

1 Reading   A Japanese space hotel

A&B 1 c, 2 g, 3 a, 4 f, 5 e, 6 b, 7 d

C 1 false   2 true   3 true
4 true   5 true   6 true
7 true   8 false   9 false
10 false

2 Making predictions

No set answers

3 Possibilities and probabilities

Sample answers only

1 *People will probably be able to stay in space hotels, but there are unlikely to be very many of them. They will cost a great deal, and will therefore be expensive to stay in.*
2 Air travel costs are unlikely to make mass tourism a thing of the past; different forms of power will probably be developed and air travel may become cheaper.
3 Belgium is very unlikely to become a major tourist destination.
4 Passports as we know them might be abolished, but there will definitely be some form of identification needed for travellers.
5 Travel agents probably won't work from home all the time, but they are likely to be able to do more from home than they do now.

4 Talking about mistakes

B 1 *If the developers hadn't built so many hotels, they wouldn't have ruined the resort.*
2 If the weather hadn't been so bad, we would have enjoyed our holiday.
3 If our brochures hadn't arrived late, we wouldn't have lost so many customers.
4 If he had had travel insurance, he wouldn't have had to pay the hospital bill himself.
5 If you had reconfirmed your ticket, we would have booked you a seat on the flight.
6 If you had discussed the problem with the representative, she would have sorted it out.

5 Mistakes and missed opportunities

1 *They shouldn't have built so many high rise hotels. If they had planned the development more carefully, they wouldn't have spoiled the resort.*
2 They shouldn't have allowed the hotels to employ foreigners. If they had insisted on hiring local staff, unemployment would have gone down.
3 They should have controlled the fishing industry. If they had limited catches they would have preserved fish stocks.
4 They shouldn't have let the hotels use so much water. If they had controlled the water supply, they would have protected the local farmers.
5 They shouldn't have allowed foreign companies into the country. If they had kept them out, it would have enabled local hotels to succeed.

6 Vocabulary   Tourism and the environment

1 *developing country*   2 ozone layer
3 endangered species   4 air pollution
5 environmentally friendly 6 waste disposal
7 water conservation   8 local materials

7 Reading   Exodus and the enviroment

1 *effects*   2 sound   3 in
4 offering   5 upon   6 cope
7 character   8 rather   9 individual
10 dispose   11 recruited   12 expense
13 interest   14 blend   15 respect
16 retain

8 Word and preposition combinations

1 apologize for
2 on holiday
3 aware of
4 disadvantage of
5 angry about
6 pay for
7 rise in

8 cause of
9 invitation to
10 interested in

11 delighted with
12 famous for
13 afraid of
14 depend on

15 look after
16 cheque for
17 complaints about
18 think about